Bold Baby Crochet

30 Modern & Colorful Projects for Baby

Dedri Uys

BARRON'S

Contents

Bold Baby Crochet

A Quantum Book

Copyright © 2017 Quantum Books Ltd
First edition for North America published in 2017 by
Barron's Educational Series, Inc.

All inquiries should be addressed to:
Barron's Educational Series, Inc.
250 Wireless Boulevard
Hauppauge, New York 11788
www.barronseduc.com

ISBN: 978-1-4380-0951-3
Library of Congress Control Number: 2016953372
QUMBOBB

This book was conceived, designed, and produced by:
Quantum Books Ltd
6 Blundell Street
London N7 9BH
United Kingdom

Publisher: Kerry Enzor
Editorial: Charlotte Frost and Julia Shone
Designer: Tokiko Morishima
Technical Consultant: Therese Chynoweth
Photographer: Simon Pask
Production Manager: Zarni Win

Printed in China by 1010 Printing International Ltd
9 8 7 6 5 4 3 2 1

Disclaimer
The projects in this book have been designed with
babies and toddlers in mind. Three dimensional pieces
are crocheted seamlessly or securely fastened in place.
Buttons, beads, sequins, and other plastic components
have been avoided as often as possible. When making
a project the authors and publisher urge the readers to
ensure that all elements are securely joined and that there
are no components that may become a choking hazard.
Babies and toddlers should be supervised at all times when
wearing, using, or playing with the projects contained in this
book. Because there is always a risk involved, the author
and publisher are not responsible for any adverse effects
or consequences resulting from the making of any of the
projects and please do not use this book if you are unwilling
to assume the risk. The author and publisher expressly
disclaim responsibility of any adverse effects arising from the
use or application of the information contained in this book.

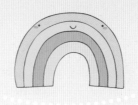

Introduction

I firmly believe that there is no greater gift for a baby than an item handmade with love. When I had my first son, a friend of ours made him a little octopus toy out of an old T-shirt. I cherished that toy right up until the day we lost it on an outing. There was something so comforting and special about the fact that she had taken the time to create a gift. It spoke of love and carried meaning.

This book is full of colorful projects for babies, each specially chosen for its vibrancy and texture. So whether you are looking for clothing, storage, or toys, you are sure to find something that says "love" to both baby and baby's parents.

The patterns are rated from easy to advanced, and the techniques section covers everything you need to know to get started—beginning with how to hold your hook and ending with how to finish your projects.

I hope that you enjoy this book and that you find the perfect project for you!

Dedri

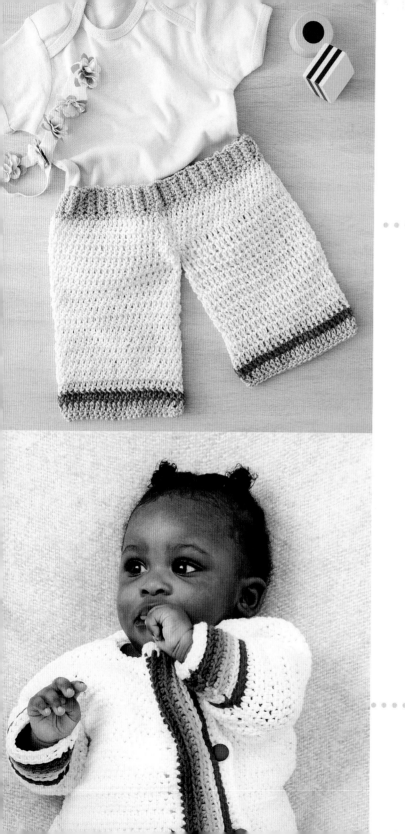

COLORFUL CLOTHING

Rainbow Band Booties

The bright stripes on these booties will add a splash of color to any outfit. Follow the stripe combination used in the pattern, or use shades of a single color for an ombré effect.

YOU WILL NEED

Worsted weight
50% merino/25% acrylic/
25% microfiber
(115 yds/105 m, 1.75 oz/50 g)

* 1 ball of beige (A)
Small amounts in the
following colors:
turquoise (B), bright green (C),
red (D), yellow (E), pink (F)

EQUIPMENT

* US G-6 (4 mm) crochet hook
* Tapestry needle

GAUGE

17 sts and 13 rows = 4" (10 cm) in
half double crochet

SIZE

Size: 0–6 months
Ankle circumference: 5" (13 cm)
Foot length from heel: 3.5" (9 cm)

TO MAKE

Sole

Round 1: With A, ch 9, work 3 dc in third ch from hook, 1 dc in each of next 5 ch, 7 dc in last ch, turn piece with opposite side of ch at top, 1 dc in each of next 5 ch, 3 dc in last ch, join with a sl st in top of beg-ch. (23 sts)

Round 2: Ch 2, 2 dc in each of next 3 sts, 1 dc in next 5 sts. 2 dc in each of next 7 sts, 1 dc in next 5 sts, 2 dc into each of next 3 sts, join with a sl st in top of first dc. (36 sts) Fasten off.

Upper

Round 1: Join A with a sl st in edge, ch 1, work BPhdc in each st around, join with a sl st in top of first BPhdc. (36 sts)

Round 2: Ch 1, sc in each st around, join with a sl st in top of first sc.

Round 3: Ch 1, sc in first 10 sts, hdc2tog 3 times, hdc in next 4 sts, hdc2tog 3 times, sc in next 10 sts, join with a sl st in top of first sc. (30 sts remain)

Round 4: Ch 1, sc in next 8 sts, hdc in next st, dc2tog 6 times, hdc into next st, sc in next 8 sts, sl st in top of first sc. (24 sts remain)

Round 5: Ch 1, sc in next 9 sts, sc2tog, hdc2tog, sc2tog, sc in next 9 sts, join with a sl st in top of first sc. (21 sts remain)

Leg

Round 6–10: Ch 1, sc in each st around, join with a sl st in top of first sc.
  Fasten off. Weave in all ends.

Stripes

Stripe 1: With B and RS facing, work a round of sl st between rounds 5 and 6. Fasten off.

Stripe 2: With C and RS facing, work a round of sl st between rounds 6 and 7. Fasten off.

Stripe 3: With E and RS facing, work a round of sl st between rounds 7 and 8. Fasten off.

Stripe 4: With D and RS facing, work a round of sl st between rounds 8 and 9. Fasten off.

Stripe 5: With F and RS facing, work a round of sl st between rounds 9 and 10. Fasten off.

Stripe 6: With B and RS facng, work a round of sl st in top of round 10. Fasten off.

FINISHING

Cut a strand of B. Thread strand under hdc2tog at center of round 5, then tie in a bow.
  Weave in remaining ends.

Gumdrops Pullover

This lightweight sweater is perfect for blustery spring or fall days. Made from an acrylic/cotton blend, it breathes well and is warm without being too heavy.

YOU WILL NEED

Worsted weight
50% cotton/50% acrylic
(175 yds/160 m, 3.5 oz/100 g)

* 2 balls of baby blue (A)
* 1 ball in the following colors:
forest green (B), orange (C),
cobalt (D), gold (E), claret (F)

EQUIPMENT

* US H-8 (5 mm) crochet hook
* US G-6 (4 mm) crochet hook
* 3 locking stitch markers
* Tapestry needle

GAUGE

13 sts and 8 rows = 4" (10 cm) in
double crochet with US H-8 (5 mm)

SIZE

Size: 6 months [12 months, 18 months]
Chest circumference: 21 [21,
22¼]" (53.5 [53.5, 56.5] cm)
Length: 11 [12, 12]"
(28 [30.5, 30.5] cm)
Shown in size 6 months.

TO MAKE

Gumdrop Stitch
(multiple of 3 sts + 2)

Round 1a (RS): Turn, sl st in first st, ch 1, place A on a removable stitch marker. Join next contrasting color with sl st in next st, ch 2 (counts as dc), dc in next st, *ch 1, skip next st, dc in next 2 sts; repeat from * around, ch 1, keeping loop on st marker and working yarn at WS, join with a sl st in top of beg-ch 2 of same color, fasten off contrasting color.

Round 1b (RS): Return A to crochet

SPECIAL STITCHES

* BPdc (see page 114)
* FPdc (see page 114)
* V-st: Dc, ch 1, dc in indicated stitch or space.

hook and pull it forward under the ch-sp from round 1a; the working loop should now be in front, with yarn in back. Working over the chains from round 1a, ch 3 (counts as dc, ch 1), dc in same st, V-st in each skipped st of previous round, join with a sl st in second ch of beg-ch.

Round 2 (WS): Ch 1, turn, hdc in first 2 dc from round 1a, *sc in next ch-sp from round 1b, hdc in next 2 dc from round 1a; repeat from * to last ch-sp from round 1b, sc in last ch-sp, join with a sl st in top of first hdc. Repeat rounds 1a–2 for pattern.

Cuffs (make 2)

Foundation ch: With A and smaller crochet hook, loosely ch 18 [18, 18], join with a sl st in first ch to form a ring, being careful not to twist chain.

Round 1 (RS): Ch 3 (counts as dc), dc in back bar of next ch and each ch around, join with a sl st in top of beg-ch.

Round 2: Ch 2 (counts as BPdc), *FPdc around next st, BPdc around next st; repeat from * to last st, FPdc around last st, join with a sl st in top of beg-ch.

Repeat last round 1 more time.

Change to larger crochet hook.

Next round (WS): Ch 1, turn, sc in each st around, join with sl st in top of first sc. Do not fasten off.

Arms (make 2)

Continuing from cuffs.

Rounds 1a and 1b (RS): With B, work rounds 1a and 1b of Gumdrop St.

Round 2 (WS): Ch 1, turn, 2 hdc in first dc, hdc in next dc, continue from * in round 2 of Gumdrop Stitch Pattern, up to last 2 dc from round 1a, hdc in next dc, 2 dc in next dc, sc in last ch-sp, join with a sl st in top of first hdc.

Round 3a (RS): Turn, sl st in first st, place A on removable st marker, skip next st, join C with a sl st in next st, ch 2 (counts as dc), dc in next

in top of beg-ch. Fasten off.

Round 5b (RS): Return A to hook and pull it forward under the ch-sp from round 5a; ch 2 (counts as dc), V-st in each remaining skipped st from previous round, join with a sl st in second ch of beg-ch.

Round 6 (WS): Ch 1, turn, hdc in next dc from round 5a, *sc in next ch-sp from round 5b, hdc in next 2 dc from round 5a; repeat from * to last ch-sp, sc in next ch-sp from round 5b, hdc in next dc from round 5a, sc in last st from round 5b, join with a sl st in top of first hdc.

Round 7a (RS): Turn, sl st in first st, ch 1, place A on removable st marker, join E with a sl st in next st, ch 2 (counts as dc), dc in same st, *ch 1, skip next st, dc in next 2 sts; repeat from * to last 2 sts, ch 1, skip next st, 2 dc in next st, ch 1, keeping A and working yarn from previous round at WS, join with a sl st in top of beg-ch. Fasten off E.

Round 7b (RS): Work round 1b of established pattern.

Round 8 (WS): Work round 2 of established pattern. (24 sts)

Round 9a (RS): With F, work round 1a of established pattern.

Round 9b (RS): Work round 1b of established pattern.

Round 10 (WS): Working into dc from round 9a, and ch-sp from round

st, continue from * in round 1a of Gumdrop st to last st, skip last st, do not join, fasten off B.

Round 3b (RS): Pick up A, ch 3, 2 dc in next st, V-st in each skipped st from previous round to last skipped st, 2 dc in last skipped st, join.

Round 4 (WS): Ch 1, sc in first 2 sts, * hdc in next 2 dc from round 3a, sc in next ch-sp from round 3b; repeat from

* 4 more times, hdc in next 2 dc from round 3a, sc in last 3 dc from round 4b, join.

Round 5a (RS): Turn, sl st in first st, ch 1, place A on removable st marker, join D with a sl st in next st, ch 2 (counts as dc), *ch 1, skip next st, dc in next 2 sts; rep from * to last 2 sts, ch 1, skip next st, dc in next st, ch 1, keeping A at WS, join D with a sl st

9b, ch 1, turn, 2 hdc in first dc, hdc in next dc *sc in next ch-sp, hdc in next 2 dc; repeat from * to last 2 ch-sps, sc in next ch -sp, hdc in next dc, 2 hdc in next dc, sc in last ch-sp, join with a sl st in top of first hdc. (26 sts)

Sizes 6 months only

Round 11: Turn, sl st in first st, ch 1, sc in each st around, join with a sl st in top of first sc. (26 sts)

Size 12 months only

Round 11: Turn, sl st in first st, ch 1, sc in each st to last st, 1 sc in last st, join. (26 sts)

Round 12: Turn, sl st in first st, ch 3 (counts as dc), dc in each st to last st, 2 dc in last st, join with a sl st in top of beg-ch. (1 st increased) (27 sts)

Sizes 18 months only

Round 11: Turn, sl st in first st, ch 3 (counts as dc), dc in each st to last st, 2 dc in last st, join. (27 sts)

Round 12: Ch 3 (counts as dc), turn, dc in each st to last st, 2 dc in last st, join with a sl st in top of beg-ch. (1 st increased).

Repeat last round once. (29 sts)

All sizes

Next round: Turn, sl st in first st, ch 3 (counts as dc), dc in each st around, join with a sl st in top of beg-ch.

Repeat last round 0 [1, 0] more time(s). Fasten off at end of last round. Piece should measure approximately 5 [6, 6¼]" (12.5 [15, 16] cm) from beg.

Turn work, skip first st, place marker in next st. Set aside.

Body

Foundation ch: With A and smaller crochet hook, loosely ch 72 [72, 74]. Do not join.

Row 1 (RS): Beg in fourth ch from hook, dc in back bar only of each ch across, join with a sl st in top of beg-ch, being careful not to twist. (70 [70, 72] sts)

Round 2: Ch 2 (counts as BPdc), *FPdc around next st, BPdc around next st; rep from * to last st, FPdc around last st, join with a sl st in top of beg-ch.

Change to larger crochet hook.

Size 18 months only

Next round: Ch 1, turn, sc in each st around, join with a sl st in top of first sc.

Sizes 6 months [12 months] only

Next round: Ch 1, turn, sc in each st to last 2 sts, sc2tog, join with a sl st in top of first sc. (69 sts remain)

All sizes

Working in Gumdrop st, work rounds 1a–2 five times, working contrasting colors as follows: B, C, D, E, then F.

Sizes 6 months only

Next round: Turn, sl st in first st, ch 3 (counts as dc), dc in next st and in each st to last 2 sts, dc2tog, join with a sl st in top of beg–ch. (68 sts remain)

Size 12 months only

Next round: Ch 1, turn, sc2tog, sc in each st around, join with a sl st in top of sc2tog. (68 sts remain)

Size 18 months only

Next round: Ch 1, turn, sc in next st and each st around. (72 sts)

All sizes

Next round: Turn, sl st in first st, ch 3 (counts as dc), dc in each st around.

Repeat last round 0 [2, 2] more times. Piece should measure approximately 5½ [6½, 6½]" (14 [16.5, 16.5] cm) from beg.

Yoke

Joining round: With RS of body facing, sl st in first 2 sts, ch 2 (does not count as dc), skip st at base of ch, dc in next 29 [29, 31] sts, dc2tog, place marker in last st made, with RS of sleeve facing, dc2tog in marked st and next st on sleeve, remove marker, dc in next 20 [21, 23] sts, dc2tog, place marker in last st made, leaving remaining sleeve sts unworked, continue along body, skip next 2 sts, dc2tog, dc in next 28 [28, 30] sts, dc2tog, place marker in last st, with RS of remaining sleeve facing, dc2tog in marked st and next st, dc in next 20 [21, 23] sts, dc2tog, leave remaining 2 sleeve sts and 1 body st(s) unworked, join with a sl st to first dc on body. (104 [106, 114] sts; 30 [30, 32] sts each for front and back, and 22 [23, 25] sts for each sleeve).

Decrease round: Turn, sl st in first st, ch 2 (does not count as st), skip first st, *dc in each st to 2 sts before marker, dc2tog, move marker to dec st, dc2tog; rep from * twice more, dc to last 2 sts, dc2tog, join with a sl st in top of first dc. (8 sts decreased)

Repeat decrease round 5 [5, 6] more times. (56 [58, 58] sts remain; 18 sts remain each for front and back, and 10 [11, 11] sts remain for each sleeve).

Shape Front Neck

Sizes 6 months [12 months] only

Next round: Turn, sl st in first st, ch 2 (does not count as a st), skip first dc, *dc in each st to 2 sts before marker, dc2tog, remove marker, dc2tog**, dc in next 3 sts, hdc in next 3 sts, sc in next 2 sts, hdc in next 3 sts, dc in next 3 sts, dc2tog, remove marker, dc2tog; repeat from * to **, dc in each st to last 2 sts, join with a sl st in first dc. (48 [50] sts remain)

Size 18 months only

Decrease round: Turn, sl st in first st, ch 2 (does not count as a st), skip first dc, *dc in each st to 2 sts before marker, dc2tog, remove marker, dc2tog; repeat from * once more, dc in next 3 sts, hdc in next 3 sts, sc in next 2 sts, hdc in next 3 sts, dc in next 3 sts, dc2tog, remove marker, dc2tog, dc in each st to last 2 sts, dc2tog, join with a sl st in first dc. (50 sts remain).

All sizes

Change to smaller crochet hook.

Round 1 (WS): Turn, sl st in first st, ch 3 (counts as dc), dc in each st around, join with a sl st in top of beg-ch.

Round 2 (RS): Turn, sl st in first st, ch 2 (counts as BPdc), *FPdc around next st, BPdc around next st; repeat from * to last st, FPdc around last st, join with a sl st in top of beg-ch.

FINISHING

Weave in ends. Block to measurements (see page 121). Sew underarm seams.

(see page 121)

Buttons (make 5)

Round 1 (WS): With smaller crochet hook and B, ch 2, 6 sc in second ch from hook, join with a sl st in first sc. (6 sts)

Round 2 (RS): Turn, ch 1, sc in first st, *ch 1, sc in next st; repeat from * around. Fasten off with an invisible join, leaving a long tail for sewing.

Make 4 more buttons, 1 each with colors C, D, E, and F.

Sew buttons securely to left front yoke along raglan line (this is the diagonal line that joins the sleeve to the rest of the pullover. Use photo as a guide), using running st or back st along edges.

Ombré Socks

These ombré socks are a modern take on traditional white socks. They are great for using up leftover yarns and turning them into something pretty and functional!

YOU WILL NEED

Sport weight
55% wool/33% microfiber/
12% cashmere
(137 yds/125 m, 1.75 oz/50 g)

1 ball in the following colors:
* **Blue socks:** white (A), baby blue (B), sky blue (C), and electric blue (D)
* **Yellow socks:** white (A), pale yellow (B), gold (C), bright yellow (D)

EQUIPMENT
* US E-4 (3.5 mm) crochet hook
* Stitch markers
* Tapestry needle

GAUGE
24 sts and 24 rounds = 4" (10 cm)
in single crochet

SIZE
Size: 6–12 months [1–3 years]
Foot circumference: 4 [10½]"
(5.5 [14] cm)
Foot length from heel: 4 [5]"
(10 [13] cm)

TO MAKE

Cuff
Foundation ch: With A, ch 11.
Row 1 (RS): Beg in second ch from hook, sc in each ch across, ch 1, turn. (10 sts)
Row 2 (WS): Ch 1 (doesn't count as sc) sc in back loop only across, ch 1, turn. (10 sts)
Rows 3–26 [30]: Repeat row 2. Mark last stitch of last row. Piece should measure approximately 1½ [1¾]" (3.75 [4.5] cm).
Joining row: Holding both short ends together, *sl st in beg-ch and front loop only of last row; repeat from * to end. Fasten off.

Ankle
Round 1: With B, join with a sl st in marked last st of cuff, sc in same st, sc in each row around, join with a sl st in first sc. (26 [30] sts)
Round 2: Ch 1 (does not count as sc), sc in first st, ch 1, skip 1 st, *sc in next st, ch 1, skip 1 st; repeat from * 11 [13] more times, join with a sl st in first sc.
Round 3: Ch 2, skip first ch-1 sp, *sc in next ch- 1 sp, ch 1, skip 1 st; repeat from * 11 [13] more times, sc in last ch-1 sp, join with a sl st in first ch of beg-ch.
Round 4: Ch 1, *sc in next ch-1 sp, ch 1, skip 1 st; repeat from * 12 [14] more times, join with a sl st in beg-ch.
Rounds 5–7: Repeat rounds 3–5.
Round 8: Repeat round 4. Fasten off.

Foot
Round 9: Join C with a sl st in ch-1 sp after join of last round, *sc in same

ch-1 sp, ch 1, skip 1 st; repeat from * 5 [6] more times, sc in next ch-1 sp, ch 13 [15], skip 13 [15] sts, join with a sl st in first sc.

Round 10: Ch 2, *sc in ch-1 sp, ch 1, skip 1 st; repeat from * 5 [6] more times, (sc in ch, ch 1, skip 1 ch) 6 [7] times, sc in last ch, join with a sl st in first ch.

Repeat rounds 4 and 5 two [three] times. Fasten off.

Next round: Join D with a sl st in ch-1 sp after join of last round; repeat round 2.

Next round: Repeat round 3.

Repeat rounds 4 and 5 twice.

Toe

Note: Work the toe in a spiral without joining at the end of each round.

Next row: Ch 1 (does not count as sc), sc in each st around, do not join.

Size 6–12 months only

Decrease round 1: Sc2tog, *2 sc, sc2tog; repeat from * 5 more times. (19 sts remain)

Decrease round 2: Sc, *sc in next st, sc2tog; repeat from * 5 more times. (13 sts remain)

Decrease round 3: Sc, *sc2tog; repeat from * 5 more times. (7 sts remain)

Size 1–3 years only

Decrease round 1: *3 sc, sc2tog; repeat from * 5 more times. (24 sts remain)

Decrease round 2: *2 sc, sc2tog; repeat from * 5 more times. (18 sts remain)

Decrease round 3: *Sc, sc2tog; repeat from * 5 more times. (12 sts remain)

Decrease round 4: *Sc2tog; repeat from * 5 more times. (6 sts remain)

All sizes

Fasten off. Thread tail through top of remaining sts and pull to close hole.

Heel

Round 1: Join A anywhere in heel, ch 1, work 26 (30) sc around, join with a sl st in top of first sc. (26 [30] sts)

Round 2: Ch 1 (does not count as sc), sc in next 2 sts, *sc2tog, 4 [5] sc; repeat from * 3 more times, join with a sl st in first sc. (22 [26] sts remain)

Round 3: Ch 1 (does not count as sc), sc in next 2 sts, *sc2tog, 3 [4] sc; repeat from * 3 more times, join with a sl st in first sc. (18 [22] sts remain)

Round 4: Ch 1 (does not count as sc), sc in next 2 sts, *sc2tog, 2 [3] sc; repeat from * 3 more times, join with a sl st in first sc. (14 [18] sts remain)

Size 1–3 years only

Round 5: Ch 1 (does not count as sc), sc in next 2 sts, *sc2tog, 2 sc; repeat from * 3 more times, join with a sl st in first sc. (14 sts remain)

All sizes

Fasten off, leaving a long tail for seam.

FINISHING

Fold heel with 7 sts on each side, and folds at sides of heel. Use long tail to weave sts together. Fasten off. Weave in ends.

STASH BUSTING
WITH SOCKS

These cute socks are the perfect
way to use up small amounts of
yarn in your yarn stash. Any DK-
Sport-weight yarn may be used with
the same gauge and patterns. The
Sport-weight yarn will produce
socks with a lighter fabric. So why
not look at your stash and explore
the world of color?

SAFETY FIRST

Beads can be a choking hazard for small children. If you decide to sew beads to this playsuit, make sure to securely attach them. Do not leave the baby unattended.

Little Flowers Playsuit

This dainty and elegant playsuit is the perfect project for newborn and milestone photos with your favorite professional photographer.

YOU WILL NEED

Worsted weight
77% alpaca/23% silk
(153 yds/140 m, 0.88 oz/25 g)

* 1 [2] ball of white
* Small amounts of lace weight yarn, 4 colors of choice for flowers

EQUIPMENT

* US H-8 (5 mm) crochet hook
* US G-6 (4 mm) crochet hook
* US D-3 (3.25 mm) crochet hook
* Tapestry needle
* 4 small beads (optional)

GAUGE

15 sts and 10 rows = 4" (10 cm) in half double crochet

SIZE

Size: Newborn [6 months]
Hip circumference: 11¾ [13¼]" (30 [33.5] cm)
Length, including edgings: approximately 16 [19¾]" (40.5 [50] cm)
Shown in size Newborn.

TO MAKE

Foundation ch: With largest crochet hook and main color yarn, ch 44 [50], join with a sl st in first ch. Do not twist.

Round 1: Ch 1 (does not count as hdc), hdc in each st around, join with a sl st in first hdc.

Repeat round 1 until piece measures 8 [10¼]" (20.5 [26] cm) from beg.

Legs

Round 1: Ch1 (does not count as hdc), 22 [25] hdc, join with a sl st in first hdc, leaving remaining sts unworked for second leg. (22 [25] sts)

Round 2: Ch 1 (does not count as hdc), hdc in each st around, join with a sl st in first hdc.

Repeat round 2 until leg measures 6½ [8]" (16.5 [20.5] cm).

Leg Edging

Size Newborn only

Next round: Ch 1, skip next st, sl st in next st, *skip 1 st, 5 dc in next st, skip 1 st, sl st in next st; repeat from * 3 more times, skip 1 st, 5 dc in next st, skip 2 sts, sl st in first sl st of round. [5 shells] Fasten off.

Size 6 months only

Next round: Ch 2 (counts as dc), 2 dc in same st, *skip 1 st, sl st in next st, skip 1 st, 5 dc in next st; repeat from * 4 more times, skip 1 st, sl st in next st, skip 2 sts, 2 dc in base of beg-ch, join with a sl st in top of beg-ch. [6 shells] Fasten off.

Both sizes

Second Leg

With largest crochet hook, join off white in next st after first leg with a sl st.

Round 1: Ch 1 (does not count as hdc), 22 [25] hdc, join with a sl st in first hdc. (22 [25] hdc)

Repeat round 1 until left measures 6½ [8]" (16.5 [20.5] cm).

Work edging in same way as first leg. Fasten off.

Top Edging

With largest crochet hook, join off white on side edge of foundation ch.

Size Newborn only

Next round: Ch 2 (counts as dc), 2 dc in same st, *skip 1 st, sl st in next st, skip 1 st, 5 dc in next st; repeat from * 9 more times, skip 1 st, sl st in next st, skip 1 st, 2 dc in base of beg-ch, join with a sl st in top of beg-ch. (11 shells) Fasten off.

Size 6 months only

Next round: Ch 1, sl st in same st and in next st, ch 2 (counts as dc), 2 dc in same st, *skip 1 st, sl st in next st, skip 1 st, 5 dc in next st; repeat from * 10 more times, skip 1 st, sl st in next st, skip 1 st, 2 dc in base of beg-ch, join with a sl st in top of beg-ch. (12 shells) Fasten off.

Both sizes

Ties (make 4)

With size G-6 (4 mm) crochet hook and off white, join yarn to foundation ch 1¼ [1½]" (3 [4] cm) from side edge behind top edging, ch 50 [55]. Fasten off.

Make 3 more ties, with 2 on front and back, and on each side of pants.

FINISHING

Weave in ends.

Flowers (make 4)

With smallest crochet hook and color of choice, make a magic ring.

Round 1: Ch 1, 10 sc in ring, pull tail to tighten ring, join with a sl st in top of first sc. (10 sts)

Round 2: Ch 1, sl st in same st, 5 dc in next, *sl st in next st, 5 dc in next st; repeat from * 3 more times, join with a sl st in first sl st. (5 petals)

Fasten off, leaving a long tail.

Using tails, sew flowers to playsuit evenly spacing flowers across front. If using, sew beads to center of flowers.

Weave in remaining ends.

Colorful Cardigan

The stylish asymmetric front band and bright rainbow cuffs add a fun twist to this classic cardigan design.

YOU WILL NEED

DK weight
60% cotton/40% acrylic
(153 yds/140 m, 1.75 oz/50 g)

* 3 balls of white (A)
* 1 ball in the following colors:
red (B), yellow (C), grass green
(D), cobalt (E), purple (F)

EQUIPMENT

* US G-6 (4 mm) crochet hook
* Removable stitch marker or
safety pin
* Tapestry needle
* Four ¾" (15 mm) buttons

GAUGE

16 sts and 13 rows = 4" (10 cm) in
half double crochet

SIZE

Size: 3–6 months [6–12 months]
Chest circumference: 20 [22]"
(51 [56] cm)
Length: 10¼ [11½]" (26 [29] cm)
Shown in size 6–12 months

TO MAKE

Back

Foundation ch: With A, ch 41 [45].
Row 1 (RS): Beg in third ch from hook
(counts as hdc), hdc in the back bump
only of each ch across, turn.
(40 [44] sts)
Row 2: Ch 2 (counts as hdc), hdc in
each st across, turn.

Repeat row 2 until piece measures
6½ [7]" (16.5 [18] cm) from beg,
ending with a RS row.

Armholes

Next row (WS): Ch 1, turn, sl st in 4
[6] sts, ch 2 (counts as hdc), hdc in each
st to last 4 [6] sts, turn. (32 sts remain)
Next row: Ch 2 (counts as hdc), hdc
in each st across, turn.

Repeat last row until armholes
measure 2¾ [3¼]" (7 [8.25] cm).

Shape Neck

Next row: Ch 2 (counts as hdc), hdc
in next 8 sts, sl st in next 14 sts, hdc
each st to end, turn. (9 sts remain for
each shoulder—do not count sl sts).
Next row: Ch 2 (counts as hdc), hdc
in next 8 sts, sl st in next 14 sts, hdc
in each st to end. Fasten off, leaving a
long tail to sew. Back measures 10.5"
[11.5"] (26.5 [29.25] cm).

Sleeves (make 2)

Foundation ch: With A, ch 25 [27].
Row 1 (RS): Beg in third ch from

hook (2 skipped ch count as hdc), hdc in the back bump of each ch across, turn. Fasten off but do not turn. (24 [26] sts)

Row 2 (RS): With RS facing, join F with a sl st in top of beg-ch, ch 2 (counts as hdc), hdc in back bar only of each st across. Fasten off, leaving a long tail for sewing. Do not turn.

Row 3 (RS): Join E and repeat row 2.

Row 4 (RS): With RS facing, join D with a sl st in top of beg-ch, (ch 2 counts as hdc) work an additional hdc in top of beg-ch, working in the back bar only, work hdc to end. Fasten off, leaving a long tail for sewing. (25 [27] sts)

Row 5 (RS): With RS facing, join C with a sl st in top of beg-ch, ch 2 (counts as hdc), working in back bar only, work hdc to last st, 2 hdc in last st. Fasten off, leaving a long tail for sewing. (26 [28] sts)

Row 6 (RS): Join B and repeat row 2.

Row 7 (RS): Join A and repeat row 4, but do not fasten off at end of row, turn. (27 [29] sts)

Row 8 (WS): Ch 2 (counts as hdc), hdc in base of beg-ch, hdc in each st to end, turn. (28 [30] sts)

Repeat row 8 four [six] more times. (32 [36] sts)

Work even until piece measures 6 [6¾]" (15 [17] cm) from beg. Fasten off, leaving a long tail for sewing.

Left Front

Foundation ch: With A, ch 19.

Row 1 (RS): Beg in third ch from hook (counts as hdc), hdc in the back bump of each ch across, turn. (18 [22] sts)

Row 2: Ch 2 (counts as hdc), hdc in each st across, turn.

Repeat row 2 until piece measures 6½ [7]" (16.5 [18] cm) from beg, ending with a RS row.

Armhole

Next row (WS): Ch 2 (counts as hdc), hdc in each st to last 4 [6] sts, turn. (14 [12] sts remain)

Next row: Ch 2 (counts as hdc), hdc in each st to end, turn.

Repeat last row until armhole measures 2¾ [3¼]" (7 [8.25] cm), ending with a WS row.

Shape Neck

Next row (RS): Ch 2 (counts as hdc), hdc in each st, to last 9 [5] sts, turn. (5 [7] sts remain for shoulder—do not count sl sts).

Next row (WS): Ch 2 (counts as hdc), hdc in each st to end, turn.

Repeat last row until armhole measures 4 [4½]" (10 [11.5] cm). Fasten off, leaving a long tail. Left front measures 10.5" [11.5"] (26.5 [29.25] cm).

Right Front

Foundation ch: With A, ch 19 [23].

Row 1 (RS): Beg in third ch from hook (counts as hdc), hdc in the back bump of each ch across, turn. (18 [22] sts)

Row 2: Ch 2 (counts as hdc), hdc in each st across, turn.

Repeat row 2 until piece measures 6½ [7]" (16.5 [18] cm) from beg, ending with a RS row.

Armhole

Next row (WS): Ch 1, sl st in each of next 4 [6] sts, ch 2 (counts as hdc), hdc in each st to end, turn. (14 [16] sts remain)

Next row: Ch 2 (counts as hdc), hdc in each st to end, turn.

Repeat last row until armhole measures 2¾ [3¼]" (7 [8.25] cm), ending with a RS row.

Shape Neck

Next row: Ch 1, sl st in next 9 sts, ch 2 (counts as hdc), hdc in each st to end, turn. (5 [7] sts remain for shoulder—do not count sl sts).

Next row: Ch 2 (counts as hdc), hdc in each st to end, turn.

Repeat last row until armhole measures 4 [4½]" (10 [11.5] cm). Fasten off, leaving a long tail. Right front measures 10.5" [11.5"] (26.5 [29.25] cm).

FINISHING

Weave in ends. Block pieces to measurements (see page 121)

With right sides facing, sew back and fronts together at shoulders.

Sew in sleeves along vertical and sl st edges of armholes.

Sew side and sleeve seams, using tails of stripe colors at cuffs to sew those sections together.

Rainbow Band

Row 1 (RS): With RS facing, join A with a sl st at bottom of right front, ch 1, sc in same st, work 35 [39] more sc evenly spaced along right front edge to neck. Fasten off. (36 [40] sts)

Row 2 (RS): Join F with a sl st in first sc of previous row, ch 2, (counts as hdc), hdc in each st across. Fasten off.

Row 3 (RS): Join E with a sl st in first hdc of previous row, ch 2 (counts as 1 hdc), hdc in back bar of each st across. Fasten off.

Row 4 (RS): Join D and repeat row 3.

Row 5 (RS): Join C and repeat row 3.

Row 6 (RS): Join B and repeat row 3.

Buttonhole row (RS): Join A, ch 2 (counts as hdc), skip 1 st, working in the back bar of each st, hdc in next 11 [12] sts, ch 1, skip 1 st, hdc in next 10 [12] sts, ch 1, skip 1 st, hdc in 10 [11] sts, ch 1, hdc in last st, place removable marker or safety pin in loop.

Weave in ends of rainbow band.

Front, Neck, and Bottom Edging

Return loop to crochet hook. Note: work this final edging row through both the front and back loops of each stitch along horizontal edges.

With RS facing and working along neck edge, work 1 hdc in space between each color row, continue around neck edge, 1 sc in each sl st or skipped st, 1 sc in each row along vertical neck edges, work 2 sc in corner st, sc down left front edge, 2 sc in corner st, 1 sc in each st of foundation ch and 1 sc in space between each color row, (1 hdc, 2 sc) in beg-ch of last row of rainbow band, work 2 sc in each ch-1 space and 1 sc in each st along right front, then 1 sc in last hdc of row, continue across end of rainbow band, sc to end of rainbow band, then join using invisible join.

With RS facing and bottom edge up, join A with a sl st in bottom edge in first row of rainbow band, sc along lower edge of rainbow band, then join using invisible join at front edge. Weave in remaining ends.

Sew buttons to left front opposite button loops.

Bright Striped Sun Hat

Absolutely adorable, the Bright Striped Sun Hat features a simple single crochet brim to protect baby's face and neck from the summer sun. Add a set of ties to secure it in place and make your baby the cutest one in town.

YOU WILL NEED

DK weight
60% cotton/40% acrylic
(153 yds/140 m, 1.75 oz/50 g)

* 2 balls of white (A)
* Small amounts in the
following colors:
red (B), bright yellow (C),
green (D), cobalt (E), purple (F)

EQUIPMENT
* US G-6 (4 mm) crochet hook
* US E-4 (3.5 mm) crochet hook
* Stitch marker
* Tapestry needle

GAUGE
16 sts and 12 rounds = 4" (10 cm)
in half double crochet

SIZE
Size: Newborn [3–6 months]
Head circumference: 14 [17]"
(35.5 [43] cm)

SPECIAL STITCHES
* Standing sc (see page 114)
* Standing hdc (see page 115)

TO MAKE

Crown

Use a stitch marker to keep track of the beginning of rounds and move the marker up as you work.

With larger crochet hook and A, make a magic ring.

Round 1: Ch 2 (counts as hdc), work 7 hdc into ring. (8 sts)

Round 2: 2 hdc in each st around. (16 sts)

Round 3: *2 hdc in next st, 1 hdc in next st; repeat from * around. (24 sts)

Round 4: *2 hdc in next st, hdc in next 2 sts; repeat from * around. (32 sts)

Round 5: *2 hdc in next st, 1 hdc in next 3 sts; repeat from * around. (40 sts)

Round 6: *2 hdc in next st, 1 hdc in next 4 sts; repeat from * around. (48 sts)

Round 7: *2 hdc in next st, 1 hdc in next 11 [5] sts; repeat from * around. (52 [56] sts)

Size Newborn only

Rounds 8–13: Hdc in each st around. Cut A and join with an invisible join at end of last round.

Size 3–6 months only

Round 8: *2 hdc in next st, 1 hdc in

next 6 sts; repeat from * around. (64 sts)

Rounds 9–15: Hdc in each st around. Cut A and join with an invisible join at end of last round.

Rainbow Band

Next round: With larger crochet hook, join B with standing hdc in back bar of any st, hdc in back bar of each st around. Cut B and join with an invisible join. (52 [64] sts)

Next round: Join C and repeat last rnd.

Next round: Join D and repeat last rnd.

Next round: Join E and repeat last rnd.

Next round: Join F and repeat last rnd.

Next round: Join A with standing sc in back bar of any st, sc in back bar of each st around. Do not join. Piece should measure approximately 5 [6¼]" (12.5 [16] cm) from center of crown.

Brim

Change to smaller hook.

Round 1: *Sc in next st, 2 sc in next st; repeat from * around. (78 [96] sts)

Rounds 2 and 3: Sc in each st around.

Round 4: *2 sc in next st, 1 sc in next 2 sts; repeat from * around. (104 [128] sts)

Rounds 5 and 6: Sc in each st around.

Round 7: *2 sc in next st, 1 sc in next 3 sts; repeat from * around. (130 [160] sts)

Rounds 8 and 9: Sc in each st around.

Round 10: Sl st in each st around. Cut A and join with an invisible join.

Weave in ends.

FINISHING

Ties (make 2, optional)

With smaller crochet hook and WS facing, join A with standing sc in any st of stripe in E on inside of hat.

Row 1: Ch 60, beg in second ch from hook and work 1 sl st in back bump of each ch back to the hat. Fasten off neatly to inside loops of hat.

Count 26 [32] sts first tie and work second tie in same way as first.

If your hat becomes misshapen, lightly block it flat (see page 121).

Citrus Diaper Cover

This bright and cheerful striped diaper cover mixes summery citrus colors
with bright white to really make the design pop!

YOU WILL NEED

DK weight
60% cotton/ 40% acrylic
(153 yds/140 m, 1.75 oz/50 g)

* 1 ball in the following colors:
bright yellow (A), white (B),
red (C), orange (D), grass green (E)

EQUIPMENT

* US G-6 (4mm) crochet hook
* Tapestry needle
* 2 x hook and loop tape
2½" (6.5 cm) long
* 2 x ½" (13 mm) buttons
(optional)
* Sewing needle and matching
thread

GAUGE

* 16 sts and 8 rows = 4" (10 cm) in
double crochet

SIZE

Size: 3 [6] months
Waist circumference:
18 [19]" (45.5 [48.5] cm)
Shown in size 3 [6] months.

TO MAKE

Back

Foundation ch: Using C, ch 43 [47].
Row 1: Beg in fourth ch from hook
(counts as dc), dc into each ch across,
turn. (41 [45] sts)
Row 2: Ch 3 (counts as dc), dc in each
st across, turn. Fasten off.
Row 3: Join B and ch 2 (counts as
hdc), hdc in each st across, turn.
Rows 4 and 5: Repeat row 3.
Fasten off.
Rows 6 and 7: Join D and repeat row
2. Fasten off at end of last row.
Row 8: Join B, ch 2, skip next st, hdc
in next st (counts as hdc2tog), hdc to
last 2 sts, hdc2tog, turn.
(39 [43] sts remain)
Row 9: Ch 2, skip next st, hdc in next
st, hdc to last 2 sts, hdc2tog, turn.
(37 [41] sts remain)
Row 10: Ch 2, skip next st, hdc in
next st, hdc to last 2 sts, hdc2tog, turn.
Fasten off. (35 [39] sts remain)
Row 11: Join A, ch 3, skip next st, dc
in next st (count as a dc2tog), dc to last
2 sts, dc2tog, turn. (33 [37] sts remain)
Row 12: Ch 3, skip next st, dc in next
st, dc to last 2 sts, dc2tog, turn. Fasten
off. (31 [35] sts remain)
Row 13: Join B, ch 2, skip next st, hdc
in next st, hdc to last 2 sts, hdc2tog,
turn. (29 [33] sts remain)
Row 14: Ch 2, skip next st, hdc in
next st, hdc to last 2 sts, hdc2tog, turn.
(27 [31] sts remain)
Row 15: Ch 2, skip next st, hdc in
next st, hdc to last 2 sts, hdc2tog, turn.
Fasten off. (25 [29] sts remain)
Row 16: Join E, ch 2, skip next st, dc
in next st, dc to last 2 sts, dc2tog, turn.

(23 [27] sts remain)

Row 17: Ch 2, skip next st, dc in next st, dc to to last 2 sts, dc2tog, turn. Fasten off. (21 [25] sts remain)

Front

Row 18: Join B, ch 1, hdc across, turn.

Rows 19 and 20: Rep row 18. Fasten off.

Row 21: Join A, ch 3, dc across, turn.

Row 22: Repeat row 21. Fasten off.

Rows 23–25: Repeat rows 18–20.

Rows 26 and 27: Repeat rows 21 and 22.

Rows 28–30: Repeat Rows 18–20.

Row 31: Join A, ch 3, dc in same st (counts as dc increase), dc to last st, 2 dc in last st, turn. (23 [27] sts)

Row 32: Ch 3, dc in same st, dc to last st, 2 dc in last st, turn. Fasten off. (25 [29] sts)

Rows 33–35: Repeat rows 18–20. Fasten off at end of last row.

Hook and Loop Tape Waistband

The waistband is worked into the sides of Rows 1–5.

Row 1: Holding piece with red stripe at top, with A and WS facing, join yarn with a sl st in bottom of white stripe, ch 1, work 10 sc along top edge, turn. (10 sts)

Row 2: Ch 1, hdc across, turn.

Repeat last row 11 [14] more times.

Fasten off.

Repeat along other side of back.

Button-closure Waistband

Work in same way as hook and loop tape waistband until 10 [13] rows have been worked.

Buttonhole row 1: Ch 2, 3 hdc, ch 2, skip next 2 sts, hdc in next st, then each st to end, turn.

Buttonhole row 2: Ch 2, 3 hdc, hdc in each ch, hdc in next st, then each st to end, turn.

Next row: Ch 1, hdc across. Fasten off.

Repeat along other side of back.

FINISHING

Edging

With A and WS facing, work 1 round of sc along all edges, working 3 sc in each corner. Fasten off.

Weave in all ends.

Sew hook portion of tape to front flap and loop portions of tape to each end of waistband.

Sew buttons to front flap under buttonholes.

Snuggly Monster Mitts

Add a little playfulness to these colorful mittens by creating a monster face! These mitts feature a drawstring tie closure to easily fit on your little one's hands.

YOU WILL NEED

DK weight
60% cotton/40% acrylic
(153 yds/140 m, 1.75 oz/50 g)

* 1 ball of white (A)
* Small amounts in the
following colors:
red (B), bright yellow (C),
green (D), cobalt (E), purple (F)

EQUIPMENT

* US G-6 (4 mm) crochet hook
* US B-1 (2.25 mm) crochet hook
* Small amounts of embroidery
floss in colors black, white, red,
and purple
* Tapestry needle

GAUGE

16 sts and 12 rounds = 4" (10 cm)
in half double crochet

SIZE

Size: Newborn [3–6 months]
Hand circumference: 5 [6]"
(12.75 [15] cm)
Length: 3½ [3¾]" (9 [9.5] cm)
Shown in size Newborn.

TO MAKE

Mitts (make 2)

Round 1: With larger crochet hook and B, ch 3, work 7 [8] hdc in third ch from hook, join with a sl st in first hdc. (7 [8] sts)

Round 2: Ch 2, 2 hdc in each st around, join with a sl st in first hdc. (14 [16] sts)

Round 3: Ch 2, *2 hdc in next st, hdc in next st; repeat from * around. Cut yarn and fasten off with an invisible join. (21 [24] sts)

Round 4: Join A with standing hdc, 1 hdc in each st around.

SPECIAL STITCHES

* Standing sc (see page 114)
* Standing hdc (see page 115)
* BLO (see page 114)

Round 5: Hdc in each st around. Repeat round 5 three [four] more times. Piece should measure approximately 2¾ [3]" (7 [7.5] cm).

Cuff

Next round: Join B with standing hdc in back bar of any st, hdc in back bar each st around. Cut B and join with an invisible join. (21 [24] sts)

Next round: Join C and repeat last rnd.

Next round: Join D and repeat last rnd.

Next round: Join E and repeat last rnd.

Next round: Join F and repeat last rnd.

Next round: Join A and repeat last rnd. Weave in ends.

FINISHING

Ties (make 2)

With larger crochet hook, ch 50 [55]. Fasten off and weave in ends.

Weave tie in and out between posts of last round of cuffs. Tie in a bow.

Eyes (make 4)

Foundation ring: With smaller crochet hook and black embroidery thread, make a magic ring.

Round 1: Ch 2, work 7 hdc in ring. Cut thread and join with an invisible join. (8 sts)

Round 2: Join white embroidery thread with a standing sc, leaving a 4" (10 cm) long tail, work 1 more sc in same st, then 2 sc in each st around. Do not join. (16 sts)

Round 3: Sl st in each st around. Cut thread and join with an invisible join. Weave in all ends.

Horns (make 4)

Foundation ch: With smaller crochet hook and red embroidery thread, ch 8, leaving a 4" (10 cm) long tail.

Row 1: Beg in second ch from hook, sc in next 3 ch, hdc in next 4 chs, turn. (7 sts)

Row 2: Ch 2, hdc in 4 hdc, sc in next 3 sc, turn.

Row 3: Ch 1, sc in 3 sc, hdc in 4 hdc, turn.

Row 4: Fold in half to form a long tube, work sl st through both layers of foundation ch and last row. Fasten off.

Make 1 more horn with red embroidery thread, then 2 with purple embroidery thread.

Using long yarn tails from eyes and horns, sew pieces to mittens as shown in photo, or as desired. Weave in remaining ends.

Spring Stripes Dress

This petite, beautiful dress is perfect for the spring! Make the matching leggings on page 34 to complete the outfit.

YOU WILL NEED

Sport weight
100% cotton
(69 yds/63 m, 0.88oz/25 g)

* 3 [4] balls of lemon yellow (A)
* 1 ball in the following colors:
  coral (B), pink (C), cyan (D)

EQUIPMENT

* US E-4 (3.5mm) crochet hook
* Tapestry needle

GAUGE

16 sts and 8 rows = 4" (10 cm) in
double crochet

SIZE

Size: 3 [6] months
Chest: 15¾ [16½]" (40 [42] cm)
Length: 12 [13]" (30.5 [33] cm)

TO MAKE

Yoke

Foundation ch: With B, ch 71 [76],
join with a sl st in first ch, taking care
not to twist ch.

Round 1: Ch 3 (counts as dc), dc in
next 7 [8] ch, (dc, ch 1, dc) in next ch,
*dc in next 17 [18] ch, (dc, ch 1, dc);
repeat from * 2 more times, dc to end,
join with a sl st in beg-ch. Fasten off.
(79 [84] sts)

Round 2: Join C, ch 3 (counts as dc),
*dc to ch-1 sp, (dc, ch 1, dc) in ch-1
sp; repeat from * 3 more times, dc to
end, join with a sl st in beg-ch. Fasten
off. (87 [92] sts)

Round 3: Join D, ch 3 (counts as dc),
*dc to ch-1 sp, (dc, ch 1, dc) in ch-1
sp; repeat from * 3 more times, dc to
end, join with a sl st in beg-ch. Fasten
off. (95 [100] sts)

Round 4: Join A, ch 3 (counts as dc),
*dc to ch-1 sp, (dc, ch 1, dc) in ch-1
sp; repeat from * 3 more times, dc to
end, join with a sl st in beg-ch.
(8 sts increased)

Rounds 5–7: Repeat round 4 three
more times. Fasten off at end of last
round. (127 [132] sts; 30 [32] sts for
back, 31 [32] sts for front, 31 [32] sts
for each sleeve, and 4 ch-1 sp)

Body

Round 8: With RS facing, fold yoke
so first ch-1 space and second ch-1 sp
meet, join A with a sl st through both
ch-sps, ch 3 (counts as dc), dc to 1 st
before next ch-1 sp, ch 3, sl st in next
st, line up third ch-1 sp with fourth
ch-1 sp, sl st through both ch-sps, ch
3, dc to end, join with a sl st in beg-ch.
(63 [66] sts)

Round 9: Ch 3 (counts as dc), dc in each st around, join with a sl st in beg-ch. Repeat round 9 four [six] times.

Increase round: Ch 3 (counts as dc), dc in next 5 [4] sts, 2 dc in next st, *dc in each of next 6 [5] sts, 2 dc in next st; repeat from * around, join with a sl st in beg-ch. (72 [77] sts)

Work 1 round even.

Increase round: Ch 3 (counts as dc), dc in next 7 [5] sts, 2 dc in next st, *dc in next 8 [6] sts, 2 dc in next st; repeat from * around, join with a sl st in beg-ch. (80 [88] sts) Work 1 round even.

Increase round: Ch 3 (counts as dc), dc in next 8 [6] sts, 2 dc in next st, *dc in next 9 [7] sts, 2 dc in next st; repeat from * around, join with a sl st in beg-ch. (88 [99] sts)

Work even until piece measures 8¼ [9¼]" (21 [23.5] cm) from armhole. Fasten off.

Next round: Join C, ch 1, 1 fpsc around the post of first st, *1 bpsc around the post of the next st, 1 fpsc around the post of the next st; Rep from * around, join with a sl st in beg sc.

Last round: 1 bpsc around the post of first st, *1 fpsc around the post of the next st, 1 bpsc around the post of the next st. Rep from * around, join with a sl st in beg sc. (88 [99] sts)

FINISHING

Weave in ends. Block to measurements.

Spring Stripes Leggings

This adorable pair of leggings will look great teamed with a cute pastel top or under the matching dress on page 32.

YOU WILL NEED

Sport weight
100% cotton
(69 yds/63 m, 0.88oz/25 g)

∗ 2 balls of lemon yellow (A)
∗ 1 ball in the following colors:
pink (B), cyan (C), coral (D)

EQUIPMENT

∗ US E-4 (3.5mm) crochet hook
∗ Tapestry needle

GAUGE

20 sts and 18½ rows = 4" (10 cm)
in single crochet
16 sts and 8 rows = 4" (10 cm) in
double crochet

SIZE

Size: 3 [6] months
Waist: 18 [19]" (45.5 [48.5] cm)
Length: 13 [14]" (33 [35.5] cm)

TO MAKE

Waistband

Foundation ch: With B, ch 11.
Row 1: Beg in second ch from hook, sc in each ch across, turn. (10 sts)
Row 2: Ch 1, sc in first st, sc in back loop of next 8 sts, sc in last st, turn.
Row 3-84 [88]: Rep row 2.
Joining row: Holding piece with last row and foundation ch even, work sl st through edge of foundation ch to end of row, being careful not to twist work.

Hips

Turn piece with one long edge at top.
Round 1: Ch 1, work 84 [88] sc evenly around, join with a sl st in first sc. Fasten off. (84 [88] sts)
Round 2: Join A, ch 3 (counts as dc), 10 [9] dc, 2 dc in next st, *11 [10] dc, 2 dc in next st; repeat from * 4 [6] more times, dc to end, join with a sl st in beg-ch. (90 [96] sts)
Round 3: Ch 3 (count as dc), dc each st around, join with a sl st in in beg-ch.
Rounds 4–7: Rep round 3. Piece should measure 3¼" (8.5 cm) from waistband.

First Leg

Dividing round: Ch 3 (count as dc), dc into each of next 44 [47] sts, join with a sl st in beg-ch, leaving remaining 45 [48] sts unworked. (45 [48] sts)

Next round: Ch 3 (count as dc), dc in each st around, join with a sl st in beg-ch.

Continue even until leg measures 6 [7]" (15 [18] cm), or approximately 1¾" (4.5 cm) short of desired length. Fasten off A at end of last round.

Next round: Join C, ch 3, dc in each st around, join with a sl st in beg-ch. Fasten off.

Next round: Join D, ch 3, dc in each st around, join with a sl st in beg-ch. Fasten off.

Next round: Join B, ch 3, dc in each st around, join with a sl st in beg-ch.

Next round: Ch 1, sc in each st around, join in beg sc with an invisible join. Fasten off.

Second Leg

Join A to remaining sts with a sl st, leaving a 12" (30.5 cm) long tail. Work second leg in same way as first.

FINISHING

Weave in ends. Using long tail from second leg, sew crotch closed. Block to measurements (see page 121).

Walk in the Park Hoodie

This soft and snuggly hoodie is the perfect weight for playing outside on a chilly fall evening. Mainly worked in double crochet, it's quick and easy to make!

YOU WILL NEED

Worsted weight
100% acrylic
(170 yds/155 m, 3.5 oz/100 g)

* 2 balls of cornflower blue (A)
* 1 ball of raspberry (B)
* 1 ball of bright yellow (C)

EQUIPMENT

* US J-10 (6 mm) crochet hook
* 3 locking stitch markers
* Tapestry needle

GAUGE

11 sts and 7 rows = 4" (10 cm) in double crochet

SIZE

Size: 6 months [12 months, 18 months]
Chest circumference: 21 [21¾, 22½,]" (53.5 [55, 57] cm)
Length (hem to neck): 10¾ [11½, 12]" (27.5 [29, 30.5] cm)

TO MAKE

Body

Foundation ch: With A, loosely ch 58 [60, 62], join with a sl st in first ch to form a circle, being careful not to twist chain.

Round 1 (WS [RS, WS]): Ch 3 (counts as dc), turn, dc in back bar of each ch around, join with a sl st in top of beg-ch.

Round 2: Ch 3 (counts as dc), turn, dc in each st around, join with a sl st in top of beg-ch.

Repeat last round 10 [11, 11] more times, ending with a RS [RS, WS] round. Body should measure 6¾ [7½, 7½]" (17 [19, 19] cm) from beg.

Yoke

Round 1 (WS [WS, RS]): Turn, sl st in first 2 sts, ch 3 (counts as dc), dc in next 26 [26, 28] sts, ch 16 [16, 19] for armhole, skip next 2 [3, 2] sts, dc in next 27 [27, 29] sts; ch 16 [16, 19] for armhole, skip remaining 1 [2, 1] st(s), join with a sl st in top of beg-ch. (86 [86, 96] sts; 27 [27, 29] sts each for front and back, and 16 [16, 19] sts for each sleeve).

Round 2: Turn, sl st in first st, ch 2 (does not count as a st), dc in next ch, *dc in next 12 [12, 15] ch, dc2tog, mark last st worked, dc2tog, dc in next 23 [23, 25] sts, dc2tog**, mark last st worked, dc2tog; repeat from * to **, join with a sl st in top of first dc. (78 [78, 88] sts remain)

Round 3: Turn, sl st in first st, ch 2 (does not count as a st), dc in next st,

*dc in each st to 2 sts before marker, dc2tog, move marker to last st worked, dc2tog; repeat from * 2 more times, dc in each st to last 2 sts, dc2tog, join with a sl st in top of first dc. (8 sts decreased)

Repeat last round 4 [4, 5] more times, ending with a WS row. (38 [38, 40] sts remain; 15 sts each for front and back, and 4 [4, 5] sts for sleeves).

Fasten off and remove all markers.

Mark st 7 [7, 34] st of the last round.

All sizes

Hood

With B and RS facing, join yarn in marked st with a sl st. Remove stitch marker.

Row I (RS): Ch 3 (counts as dc), dc in each st around to last st, skip last st. Do not join. (37 [37, 39] sts remain)

Row 2: Ch 3 (counts as dc), turn, dc in each st across.

Repeat last row 11 [12, 12] times.

Shape hood

Decrease row I: Ch 3 (counts as dc), turn, dc in next 15 [15, 16] sts, dc2tog, dc in next st, dc2tog, dc in each st to end. (35 [35, 37] sts remain)

Decrease row 2: Ch 3 (counts as dc), turn, dc in next 14 [14, 15] sts, dc2tog, dc in next st, dc2tog, dc in each st to end. (33 [33, 35] sts remain)

All sizes

Fasten off, leaving a long tail for sewing. Sew top of hood together along last row.

Edging round (RS): With B and RS facing, join yarn with a sl st in skipped st at center front, work 47 [51, 51] sc evenly spaced around front of hood, join with a sl st in first sc. Fasten off.

Sleeves (make 2)

Round 1: With WS [RS, WS] facing, join A with a sl st at center of underarm, ch 3 (counts as dc), work 21 [22, 24] dc evenly spaced around armhole, join with a sl st in top of beg-ch. (22 [23, 25] sts)

Round 2: Ch 3 (counts as dc), turn, dc in next st and each st to last 2 sts, dc2tog, join with a sl st in top of beg-ch. (1 st decreased)

Round 3: Ch 3 (counts as dc), turn, dc in next st and in each st around, join.

Round 4: Turn, sl st in first st, ch 2 (does not count as a st), dc in next st and each st around, join with a sl st in top of first dc. (1 st decreased)

Round 5: Repeat round 3.

Repeat rounds 2–5 one more time. (18 [19, 21] sts remain)

Repeat round(s) 2–3 [2–4, 2–5] once more, ending with a WS round. (17 [17, 19] sts remain)

Next round (RS): Repeat round 3. Fasten off.

Pocket

Foundation ch: With C, ch 21 [21, 23].

Row 1 (WS): Beg in second ch from hook, sc in each ch across. (20 [20, 22] sts)

Row 2 (RS): Ch 1 (does not count as a st), turn, sc in each st across.

Repeat last row 0 [0, 1] time(s).

Shape Sides

Decrease row 1: Turn, sl st in first st, ch 1 (does not count as a st), sc in each st across to last st, skip last st. (18 [18, 20] sts remain). Mark first and last st of this row.

Next row: Ch 1, turn, sc in each st across.

Decrease row 2: Ch 1 (does not count as a st), turn, sc2tog, sc to last 2 sts, sc2tog. (2 sts decreased)

Repeat last 2 rows 4 [4, 5] more times. (8 sts remain).

Work 1 [1, 0] more row even.

Edgings

With RS facing and working along shaped edge only, ch 1, work 12 [12, 13] sc evenly spaced along shaped edge to marked st. Fasten off.

With C and RS facing, join yarn with a sl st in marked row on other side of pocket, working along shaped edge only, ch 1, work 12 [12, 13] sc evenly spaced along shaped edge to top of pocket. Fasten off.

FINISHING

Weave in ends. Block pieces to measurements (see page 121).

Pin pocket to center front, placing bottom of pocket at top of row 2. Sew pocket to body along top, bottom, and side edges, leaving shaped edges open.

GIFTS & TOYS

Hot Air Balloon Bunting

Add a pop of color to the wall with these fun hot air balloons. You can adjust the length of the bunting to suit your style.

YOU WILL NEED

Sport weight
100% cotton
(69 yds/63 m, 0.88 oz/25 g)

1 ball in the following colors:
red (A), gold (B), teal (C), violet
(D), sky blue (E), lime green (F)

EQUIPMENT
* US D-3 (3.25 mm) crochet hook
* US G-6 (4 mm) crochet hook
* Gray felt, approximately 12"
  (30.5 cm) by 14" (35.5 cm)
* Tapestry needle
* Upholstery needle

GAUGE
Each balloon should measure 2¾"
(7 cm) wide and 3¼" (8 cm) high
before backing

SIZE
Length: 3¼" (8 cm)
Width: 2¾" (7 cm) (widest point of balloon)
Length of felt pieces: 4" (10 cm)

TO MAKE

Balloons

Make 2 each in colors A, B, C, D, and F as follows:

Foundation ch: With smaller crochet hook, ch 9.

Row 1: Beg in second ch from hook, sc in each ch across, turn. (8 sts)

Row 2: Ch 1, sc in each st across, turn.

Row 3: Ch 1, 2 sc in first st, sc to last st, 2 sc in last st, turn. (2 sts increased)

Rows 4–9: Repeat Rows 2 and 3 three more times. (16 sts)

Row 10: Ch 1, sc in first 3 sts, hdc in next 3 sts, dc in next 4 sts, hdc in next 3 sts, sc in last 3 sts, turn.

Row 11: Ch 1, 2 sc in first st, sc to last st, 2 sc in last st, turn. (18 sts)

Row 12: Ch 1, sc in next 3 sts, hdc in next 3 sts, 2 dc in next st, dc in next 4 sts, 2 dc in next st, hdc in next 3 sts, sc in next 3 sts, turn. (20 sts)

Row 13: Ch 1, sc in next 2 sts, hdc to last 2 sts, sc in next 2 sts, turn.

Row 14: Ch 1, skip first st, sc in next 3 sts, hdc in next 3 sts, 2 dc in next st, dc in next 4 sts, 2 dc in next st, hdc in next 3 sts, sc in next 2 sts, skip next st, sc in last st, turn.

Row 15: Repeat Row 14.

Row 16: Ch 1, skip first st, sc in next 3 sts, hdc in next 3 sts, 2 dc in next st, dc in next 4 sts, 2 dc in next st, hdc in next 3 sts, sc in next 2 sts, skip next st, sl st in last st. Fasten off.

Weave in ends.

Felt Backing

Using one of the balloons to create a template, cut 10 pieces of felt to back the shapes. The felt balloon should be slightly larger than the crochet balloon (excess can be trimmed away later).

Using the upholstery needle and contrasting color yarn, sew each crochet balloon onto a piece of felt with running sts. Trim any excess felt from around the balloons.

Joining the Balloons

With 2 strands of sky blue and a US G-6 (4 mm) crochet hook, ch 80. Sl st in central stitch of last row of first balloon. *25 ch, sl st in central stitch of last row of next balloon; rep from * until all the balloons are attached, ch 80. Fasten off.

Weave in ends by folding them over onto the chain and making an overhand knot with both the chain and the ends so that the ends are incorporated in the knot. Trim the ends close to the knot.

Little Bear Rattle

This cute bear rattle is great for baby girls or boys. Not only does it entertain your baby, but it also helps to develop fine motor skills, touch, and hearing.

YOU WILL NEED

Sport weight
100% cotton
(69 yds/63 m, 0.88 oz/25 g)

* 1 ball of tan (A)
* Small amounts in the following colors: turquoise (B), cyan (C), lemon yellow (D), orange (E), rose pink (F)
Small amount of black yarn

EQUIPMENT

* US C-2 (3 mm) crochet hook,
* Fiberfill
* 1½" (3.5 cm) diameter toy rattle
* Tapestry needle

GAUGE

26 sts and 24 rounds = 4" (10 cm) in single crochet

SIZE

Head circumference: 9½" (24 cm)
Handle circumference: 4¼" (11 cm)
Length: 8" (20 cm)

TO MAKE

Ears (make 2)

Foundation ring: With A, make a magic ring.
Round 1: Ch 1, 6 sc into ring. Do not join. (6 sts)
Round 2: 2 sc in each st around. Do not join. (12 sts)
Round 3: *1 sc, 2 sc in next st; repeat from * around. Do not join. (18 sts)
Rounds 4–6: 1 sc in each st around. Join with a sl st at end of last round. Fasten off, leaving a long tail to sew.

Head

Foundation ring: With A, make a magic ring.
Round 1: Ch 1, 6 sc into ring. Do not join. (6 sts)
Round 2: 2 sc in each st around. Do not join. (12 sts)
Round 3: *1 sc, 2 sc in next st; repeat from * around. Do not join. (18 sts)
Round 4: *2 sc, 2 sc in next st; repeat from * around. Do not join. (24 sts)
Round 5: *3 sc, 2 sc in next st; repeat from * around. Do not join. (30 sts)
Round 6: *4 sc, 2 sc in next st; repeat from * around. Do not join. (36 sts)
Round 7: *5 sc, 2 sc in next st; repeat from * around. Do not join. (42 sts)
Round 8: *6 sc, 2 sc in next st; repeat from * around. Do not join. (48 sts)
Round 9: *7 sc, 2 sc in next st; repeat from * around. Do not join. (54 sts)
Round 10: *8 sc, 2 sc in next st; repeat from * around. Do not join. (60 sts)

Rounds 11–17: Sc in each st around. Do not join.

Round 18: *8 sc, sc2tog; repeat from * around. Do not join. (54 sts remain)

Round 19: *7 sc, sc2tog; repeat from * around. Do not join. (48 sts remain)

Round 20: *6 sc, sc2tog; repeat from * around. Do not join. (42 sts remain)

Round 21: *5 sc, sc2tog; repeat from * around. Do not join. (36 sts remain)

Round 22: *4 sc, sc2tog; repeat from * around. Do not join. (30 sts remain)

Sew ears to head as shown in photo, bending them slightly.

Using tapestry needle, embroider eyes with black yarn, using straight sts.

Embroider nose with F, using satin st to form an inverted triangle. Add a few sts in straight st for mouth.

Stuff head and insert rattle.

Round 23: *3 sc, sc2tog; repeat from * around. Cut A and use B to join round with a sl st in first sc. (24 sts remain)

Do not cut yarn at end of each subsequent round. Drop it to the back of work, and pick up the next color.

Round 24: With B, ch 1, sc in each st around, drop B and use C to join with a sl st in first sc.

Round 25: With C, ch 1, sc in each st around, drop C and use D to join with a sl st in first sc.

Round 26: With D, ch 1, sc in each st around, drop D and use E to join with

a sl st in first sc.

Round 27: With E, ch 1, sc in each st around, drop E and use F to join with a sl st in first sc.

Round 28: With F, ch 1, sc in each st around, drop F and use B to join with a sl st in first sc.

Rounds 29–45: Firmly stuffing handle with fiberfill every few rounds as you work; repeat rounds 24–28 three more times, then repeat rounds 24 and 25 once more. Cut all colors except C on the last repeat of that color.

Round 46: With C, *2 sc, sc2tog; repeat from * around, join with a sl st

in first sc. (18 sts remain)

Round 47: *1 sc, sc2tog; repeat from * around, join with a sl st in first sc. (12 sts remain)

Round 48: *Sc2tog; repeat from * around, join with a sl st in first sc. (6 sts remain)

FINISHING

Fasten off. Add additional fiberfill to tip of handle. Thread tail through top of remaining sts, then pull tight to close hole. Weave in ends.

Friendly Soft Toys

Soft, cuddly, and with long arms and legs, any little one will love to play with these two adorable friends. They are also perfect to give as a set.

YOU WILL NEED

Sport weight
78% cotton/22% acrylic
(142 yds/130 m, 1.75 oz/50 g)

Bunny toy: 2 balls of lilac (A)
* I ball of cream (B) and amethyst (F)
* Small amounts in the following colors: duck egg (C), pale pink (D), mint green (E)
Dog toy: 2 balls of mint green (E)
* I ball of cream (B)
* Small amounts in the following colors: lilac (A), duck egg (C), pale pink (D), amethyst (F)

EQUIPMENT
* US G-6 (4 mm) crochet hook
* Tapestry needle
* Fiberfill

GAUGE
19 sts and 21 rows = 4" (10 cm) in single crochet

SIZE
Body circumference:
15" (38 cm)
Length: 18¼" (46.5 cm)

SPECIAL STITCHES
* Loop stitch (LS) (see page 113)

TO MAKE

Back

Foundation ch: With A for Bunny, and E for Dog, ch 37.
Row I: Beg in second ch from hook, sc in each ch across, turn. (36 sts)
Rows 2–46: Ch 1, sc in each st across, turn. Fasten off at end of last row.

Front

Work same as back, leaving a long tail for sewing pieces together.

Eyes

Place marker at center of front, 16 rows from the top edge. Insert hook from front to back, 4 sts to left of marker. Holding F for Bunny, and C for Dog in back of work, yarn over and pull through a loop. Working sl st along front of pieces, work 8 sts up toward top edge, 5 sts to the left, working the first and last at an angle to a curve, then 8 sts down to same row as beginning. Fasten off and pull yarn to back.

Beg 4 sts to right of marker, work remaining eye to match.

Add eyelashes if desired, using tapestry needle and same color as eyes to embroider 2 sts per lash, using photo as a guide. Fasten off.

Muzzle (Dog only)

Foundation ch: With A, ch 12.
Round I: Beg in second ch from hook, work 10 sc, 3 sc in next st, turn piece

with remaining edge of ch up, work 10 sc, 3 sc in next st. Do not join. (26 sts)

Round 2: (10 sc, 2 sc in next st, 1 sc, 2 sc in next st) twice. Do not join. (30 sts)

Round 3: (11 sc, 2 sc in next st, 2 sc, 2 sc in next st) twice. Do not join. (34 sts)

Round 4: 11 sc, 2 sc in next st, 3 sc, 2 sc in next st, 12 sc, 2 sc in next st, 4 sc, 2 sc in next st, join with a sl st in next st. Fasten off, leaving a long tail for sewing. (38 sts)

Sew muzzle to front just below eyes.

Tongue (Dog only)

Foundation ring: With D, make a magic ring.

Row 1: Ch 1, 3 sc in ring, do not join, and turn.

Row 2: Ch 1, 2 sc in each st, turn.

Row 3: Ch 1, *1 sc, 2 sc in next st; repeat from *.

Fasten off, sew just below muzzle.

Nose

Foundation ring: With C for Bunny, and F for Dog, make a magic ring.

Row 1: Ch 1, 3 sc in ring, do not join, and turn.

Row 2: Ch 1, 3 sc, turn.

Row 3: Ch 1, 1 sc, 2 sc in next st, 1 sc, turn.

Row 4: Ch 1, 1 sc, 2 sc in next st, 2 sc in next st, 1 sc. Fasten off, leaving a long tail for sewing.

Sew nose to front as shown in photo.

Belly (Bunny only)

Foundation ch: With B, ch 13.

Round 1: Beg in second ch from hook, 11 LS, 3 LS in next st, turn piece with remaining edge of ch at top, work 10 LS, 2 LS in beg-ch. Do not join. (26 sts)

Round 2: 2 LS in next st, 10 LS, 2 LS in each of next 3 sts, 10 LS, 2 LS in each of next 2 sts. Do not join. (32 sts)

Round 3: 2 LS in each of next 2 sts, 10 LS, 2 LS in each of next 5 sts, 13 LS, 2 LS in each of next 2 sts. Do not join. (41 sts)

Round 4: 2 LS in each of next 2 sts, 16 LS, 2 LS in each of next 3 sts, 18 LS, 2 LS in each of next 2 sts, join with a sl st in next st. Fasten off, leaving a long tail for sewing. (48 sts)

Sew belly to front.

Rosy Cheeks (make 2, Bunny only)

Foundation ring: With D, make a magic ring.

Round 1: Ch 1, 6 sc into ring, join with a sl st in beg-ch. Fasten off. (6 sts)

Round 2: Join E with a sl st in first sc, ch 1, 2 sc in each st around, join with a sl st in first sc. Fasten off, leaving a long tail for sewing. (12 sts)

Sew cheeks to each side of nose.

Ears (make 2)

Foundation ring: With A for Bunny, and B for Dog, make a magic ring.

Round 1: Ch 1, 6 sc into ring. Do not join. (6 sts)

Round 2: 2 sc in each st. Do not join. (12 sts)

Round 3: *1 sc, 2 sc in next st; repeat from * around. Do not join. (18 sts)

Round 4: *2 sc, 2 sc in next st; repeat from * around. Do not join. (24 sts)

Rounds 5–23: Sc around, do not join. At end of last round, join with a sl st in next st. Fasten off.

Ear Appliqué (make 2, Bunny only)

Foundation ch: With D, ch 12 sts.

Round 1: Beg in second ch from hook, 10 sc, 3 sc in last ch, turn piece with remaining edge of ch at top, 10 sc, 1 sc in beg-ch. Do not join. (24 sts)

Round 2: Sl st to beg of round 1, ch 1, 10 sc, 2 sc in each of next 3 sts, 11 sc, join with a sl st in next st. Fasten off, leaving a long tail for sewing. (27 sts)

Sew appliqués to ears as shown in photo.

Ear Appliqué (Dog only)

Make several dots using D and C.

Foundation ring: Make a magic ring.

Round 1: Ch 1, 6 sc into ring. (6 sts)

Round 2: 2 sc in each st around, join with a sl st in next st. Fasten off, leaving a tail for sewing. (12 sts)

Sew dots randomly placed on ears.

Arms (make 2)

Foundation ring: With B, make a magic ring.

Round 1: Ch 1, 6 sc into loop, join with a sl st in first sc. (6 sts)

Round 2: Ch 1, 2 sc in each st around, join with a sl st in first sc. (12 sts)

Rounds 3–5: Ch 1, sc in each st around, join with a sl st in first sc.

Rounds 6–18: Change to A for Bunny, and E for Dog. Ch 1, sc in each st around, join with a sl st to first sc. Fasten off, leaving a long tail to sew.

Legs (make 2)

Foundation ring: With B, make a magic ring.

Round 1: Ch 1, 6 sc into loop, join with a sl st in first sc. (6 sts)

Round 2: Ch 1, 2 sc in each st around, join with a sl st in first sc. (12 sts)

Round 3: Ch 1, *1 sc, 2 sc in next st; repeat from * around, join with a sl st in first sc. (18 sts)

Rounds 4–6: Ch 1, sc in each st around, cut B. With C, join with a sl st in first sc.

Round 7: Ch 1, sc in back loop of each st around, join with a sl st in first sc.

Round 8: Ch 1, sc in each st around, join with a sl st in first sc.

Change to A for Bunny, and E for Dog. Do not cut C; carry it up along the back of work.

Rounds 9 and 10: Repeat rounds 7 and 8.

Change to D, do not cut yarn used, carry it up along the back of work.

Rounds 11 and 12: Repeat rounds 7 and 8.

Pick up C from back of work.

Rounds 13 and 14: Repeat rounds 7 and 8.

Rounds 15–26: Repeat rounds 9–14 two more times. Fasten off each yarn at end of last repeat of that color, leaving a long tail of C to sew.

Tail (Dog only)

Foundation ring: With F, make a magic ring.

Round 1: Ch 1, 6 sc into ring, join with a sl st in first sc. (6 sts)

Round 2: Ch 1, 2 sc in each st around, join with a sl st in first sc. (12 sts)

Round 3: Ch 1, *1 sc, 2 sc in next st; repeat from * around, join with a sl st in first sc. (18 sts)

Rounds 4–12: Ch 1, sc in each st around, join with a sl st in first sc.

Change to E, and do not cut F, carrying it up along the back of work.

Rounds 13–16: Repeat round 4 four times.

Drop E and pick up F.

Rounds 17–20: Repeat round 4 four times. Fasten off F at end of last round.

Pick up E.

Rounds 21–26: Repeat round 4 six times. Fasten off at end of last round, leaving a long tail to sew.

Tail (Bunny only)

Make a small pompom with F.

FINISHING

Sew front and back of body together along sides and top.

Take fiberfill and stuff Bunny's ears firmly, and Dog's ears very lightly. Sew ears to top of head as shown in photo, with Bunny's ears upward, and Dog's ears pointing downward.

Stuff arms and sew to each side of body. Stuff body and sew bottom closed. Stuff legs and sew to bottom of body.

Sew tail to lower back.

MAKING A POM POM

1. Cut out two donut-shaped rings of cardboard measuring 2.5" (6 cm) in diameter and place them back-to-back.

2. Thread a 1 m strand of yarn through the middle of the circles and start wrapping it around the rings.

3. Continue until the cardboard is completely covered with several layers of yarn.

4. Place a pair of scissors between the cardboard discs and snip the wrapped yarn all the way around.

5. Slide a piece of yarn between the discs and tie it together tight. Remove the cardboard discs.

Textured Stacking Blocks

The bright, textured surfaces make these blocks fun and intriguing toys for any baby. Mix and match the motifs on each block to create a unique game for your little one.

YOU WILL NEED

DK weight
60% cotton/40% acrylic
(153 yds/140 m, 1.75 oz/50 g)

* 1 ball in the following colors:
red (A), turquoise (B), orange (C)
lime (D), fuchsia (E), yellow (F),
dark gray (G)

EQUIPMENT

* US E-4 (3.5 mm) crochet hook
* Five 4" (10 cm) cubes of dense upholstery foam
* Bread knife or electric carving knife

GAUGE

Each side block measures slightly over 4" (10 cm)

SIZE

4⅜ x 4⅜ x 4⅜" (11 x 11 x 11 cm)

SPECIAL STITCHES

* Spike stitch (see page 116)

TO MAKE

Striped Side (make 1 for each block)

Foundation ch: With first color, ch 17.
Row 1: Beg in second ch from hook, sc in each ch across, turn. (16 sts)
Rows 2–4: Ch 1, sc in each st across. At end of last row, fasten off.
Row 5: Join next color with sc in first sc, sc in each sc across, turn.
Rows 6–8: Ch 1, sc in each st across, turn. At end of last row, fasten off.
Rows 9–16: Repeat rows 5–8 once more, changing colors every 4 rows.

Edging

Row 1: With contrasting color, join with sc in top right corner of square, (ch 2, sc) in same st, *work 12 sc evenly across edge to corner, (sc, ch 2, sc) in corner st; repeat from * 2 more times, work 12 sc evenly along remaining edge, join with a sl st in first sc. Fasten off. (14 sts on each side, and 4 corner ch-2 sp)
Row 2: Join next color with sc in any corner, ch 2, sc in same corner, *work 14 sc to next corner, (sc, ch 2, sc) in ch-2 sp; repeat from * 2 more times, work 14 sc along remaining edge, join with a sl st in first sc. Fasten off. (16 sts on each side, and 4 corner ch-2 sp)

Berry Stitch Solid Side (make 1 for each block)

Foundation ch: With desired color, ch 16.
Row 1: Beg in second ch from hook, sc in each ch across, turn. (15 sts)
Row 2: Ch 1, sc in first st, (tr in next

st, sc in next st) across, turn.

Row 3: Ch 1, sc in first st, (skip tr, 2 sc in next st) across, turn.

Rows 4, 6, 8, 10, and 12: Repeat row 2.

Row 5: Ch 1, 2 sc in first st, (skip tr, 2 sc in next st) to last st, sc in last st, turn.

Row 7: Repeat row 3.

Row 9: Repeat row 5.

Row 11: Repeat row 3.

Row 13: Repeat row 5. Fasten off.

Edging

Work edging in same way as for Striped Side.

Wavy Side (make 1 for each block)

Foundation ch: With color of choice for MC, ch 14.

Row 1: Beg in second ch from hook, sc in each ch across, turn. Fasten off. (13 sts)

Row 2: With CC1 of choice, join with a sc in first st, (skip next 2 sts, 7 tr in next st, skip next 2 sts, sc in next st) 2 times, turn. Fasten off.

Row 3: Join MC with spike stitch over first sc, (sc in next 7 sts, spike st over next st) 2 times, turn. Fasten off.

Row 4: With CC2 of choice, join with a sl st in first st, ch 4 (counts as tr), 3 tr in same st, skip next 3 sts, sc in next st, skip next 3 sts, 7 tr in next st, skip next 3 sts, spike st over next st, skip next 3

sts, 4 tr in last st, turn. Fasten off.

Row 5: Join MC with a sc in first st, sc in next 3 sts, spike st in next st, sc in next 7 sts, spike st over next st, sc in last 4 sts, turn. Fasten off.

Rows 6–9: Repeat rows 2-5.

Rows 10 and 11: Repeat rows 2 and 3.

Edging

Work edging same as for Striped side.

Ripple side (make 1 for each block)

Foundation ch: With first color, ch 21.

Row 1 (WS): Beg in second ch from hook, sc in next ch, (3 sc in next ch, sc in next 2 ch, skip next 2 ch, sc in next 2 ch), twice, 3 sc in next ch, sc in next ch, sc2tog, turn. (21 sts)

Row 2 (RS): Ch 1, skip first st, (sc in next 2 sts, 3 sc in next st, sc in next 2 sts, skip next 2 sts) twice, sc in next 2 sts, 3 sc in next st, sc in next st, sc2tog, turn. Fasten off.

Row 3: Join second color with sc2tog, sc in next st, (3 sc in next st, sc in next 2 sts, skip next 2 sts, sc in next 2 sts) twice, 3 sc in next st, sc in next st, sc2tog, turn.

Row 4: Repeat row 2.

Rows 5 and 6: With third color; repeat rows 3 and 4.

Rows 7 and 8: With fourth color; repeat rows 3 and 4.

Rows 9 and 10: With fifth color;

repeat rows 3 and 4.

Rows 11 and 12: With sixth color; repeat rows 3 and 4. Do not turn at end of last row.

Edging

Round 1: With RS facing, join remaining color with a sc in first st, (ch 2, dc) in same st, (skip next st, sc in next 3 sts, skip next st, dc in next 2 sts) 2 times, skip next st, sc in next 2 sts, skip next 2 sts, (dc, ch 2, sc) in next st to turn corner, work 12 sc evenly spaced along side, (2 sc, ch 2, 2 sc) in corner, (dc in next st, skip next st, dc in next st, skip next st, sc in next 2 sts, skip next st) twice, dc in next st, skip next st, dc in next st, skip next st, (2 sc, ch 2, sc) in corner, work 12 sts evenly along side, join with a sl st in first st. Fasten off. (14 sts on each side, with 4 corner ch-2 sp)

Round 2: With next color, work same as round 2 of Striped Side edging.

Flower Circles Side (make 2 for each block)

Foundation ring: With first color, ch 5, join with a sl st in first ch to form a ring (or make a magic ring).

Round 1 (RS): Ch 3 (counts as dc), 15 dc into ring, join with a sl st in top of beg-ch. Fasten off. (16 sts)

Round 2 (WS): Turn work. Join next color with sc in any st, tr in same st, (sc, tr) in each st around, join with a sl st in first sc. Fasten off. (16 berry sts)

Round 3 (RS): Turn work. Join next color with sc in any sc, ch 1, skip next tr, (sc in next st, ch 1, skip next tr) around, join with a sl st in first sc. Fasten off. (16 sc, 16 ch-1 sp)

Round 4 (RS): Do not turn. Join next color with a sl st in any ch-1 sp, ch 3 (counts as dc), (dc, ch 2, 2 dc) in same sp, *2 hdc in next ch-1 sp, 2 sc in next ch-1 sp, 2 hdc in next ch-1 sp, (2 dc, ch 2, 2 dc) in next ch-1 sp; repeat from * 2 more times, 2 hdc in next ch-1 sp, 2 sc in next ch-1 sp, 2 hdc in next ch-1 sp, join with a sl st in top of beg-ch. Fasten off. (10 sts on each side, and 4 corner ch-2 sp)

Round 5 (WS): Turn work. Join next color with sc in any corner ch-2 sp, (ch 2, sc) in same sp, *(tr in next st, sc in next st) 5 times, (sc, ch 2, sc) in next corner ch-2 sp; repeat from * 2 more times, (tr in next st, sc in next st) 5 times, join with a sl st in first sc. Fasten off. (12 sts on each side, and 4 corner ch-2 sp)

Round 6 (RS): Turn work. Join next color with sc in any corner ch-2 sp, (ch 2, sc) in same sp, *skip first sc, (2 sc in next sc) 6 times, (sc, ch 2, sc) in next corner ch-2 sp; repeat from * 2 more times, skip next sc, (2 sc in next sc) 6 times, join with a sl st in first sc. Fasten off. (14 sc on each side, and 4 corner ch-2 sp)

Round 7 (RS): Do not turn. Join next color with sc in any corner ch-2 sp, (ch 2, sc) in same sp, *sc in each sc to corner ch-2 sp, (sc, ch 2, sc) in ch-2 sp; rep from * 2 more times, sc in each sc to corner, join with a sl st in first sc. Fasten off. (16 sts on each side, and 4 corner ch-2 sp)

FINISHING

Weave in ends. Block each square to measurements (see page 121).

Using a bread knife or electric knife, cut foam into 4" (10 cm) cubes (some irregularities in cutting are fine since they will be covered).

Holding 2 blocks together and with color of choice, work sl st through both layers along one edge. Hold another block with a corner at seam, sl st through both layers along one edge. Continue joining blocks to form a cube, fastening off and rejoining yarn as needed, and making sure to place flower circle sides on opposite sides of cube, and leaving at least 3 adjacent edges open. Insert block of foam, then join remaining edges. Fasten off. Weave in remaining ends.

Sunny Day Headband

This cute little headband has interchangeable motifs that can be swapped to match your little one's outfit. A perfect project for using up leftover scraps of yarn.

YOU WILL NEED

Sport weight
100% cotton
(69 yds/63 m, 0.88 oz/25 g)

* 1 ball in the following colors:
cream (A), red (B),
lemon yellow (C), lime green (D),
royal blue (E)
* Small amounts in the following colors:
Cloud: sky blue (F)
Sun: bright yellow (G)

EQUIPMENT
* US C-2 (3 mm) crochet hook
* Tapestry needle

GAUGE
Not important for this pattern

SIZE
Size: 6 months
Head circumference: 17" (43 cm)
Width: 1¾" (4.5 cm)

SPECIAL STITCHES
* Standing sc (see page 114)

TO MAKE

Headband

Foundation ch: With A, loosely ch 80.
Row 1 (RS): Beg in second ch from hook, sc in each ch to end. Fasten off. (79 sts)
Row 2 (RS): Join B with a standing sc in first st, *ch 1, skip 1 st, sc in next st; rep from * to end of row. Fasten off.
Row 3 (RS): Join A with a standing sc in first st, sc in ch-1 sp, *ch 1, skip 1 st, sc in ch-1 sp; rep from * to last 2 sts, sc in ch-1 sp and last st. Fasten off.

Row 4 (RS): Join C with a standing sc in first st, *ch 1, skip 1 st, sc in ch-1 sp; rep from * to last 2 sts, ch 1, skip 1 st, sc in last st. Fasten off.
Row 5 (RS): With A, repeat row 3.
Row 6 (RS): With D, repeat row 4.
Row 7 (RS): With A, repeat row 3.
Row 8 (RS): With E, repeat row 4.
Row 9 (RS): With A, repeat row 3, but do not cut yarn, ch 1, turn.
Row 10 (WS): *Sc in next st, sc in ch-1 sp; rep from * to end. Do not cut yarn.

FINISHING
Weave in ends. Hold headband with right sides together and short ends even. With yarn from last row, and working through both layers, *sc in A at row ends, ch 1, skip next row end; rep from * to last row, sc in last row end. Fasten off.

Motifs

Cloud

Foundation ch: With F, ch 10, leaving a long tail.

Row 1: Beg in third ch from hook, dc in each ch to end, ch 1, turn. (9 sts)

Row 2: Sc in each st across, ch 1, turn.

Row 3: (Sc, hdc, dc] in next st, 2 dc in next st, (hdc, sc) in next st, sl st in next st, (hdc, dc) in next st, 3 dc in next st, sc in next st, sl st in next 2 sts, rotate piece with side edge at top, (sc, hdc, 2 dc) in side of sc, dc over post of dc, turn work with foundation ch at top, (dc, hdc) in next loop, sc in next 6 loops, sc in each ch of beg-ch, join with a sl st in next st. Fasten off, leaving a long tail.

Use tapestry needle to weave ends to middle of cloud on WS. Use long tails to sew or tie motif to headband.

Sun

Foundation: With G, make a magic ring, leaving a long tail.

Round 1: Ch 3 (counts as a dc), 15 dc into ring, join with a sl st in top of beg-ch. (16 sts)

Round 2: Sc in same sp as sl st, *ch 8, sl st into third ch from hook, ch 5, sc in next st; repeat from * 14 more times, ch 8, sl st into third ch from hook, ch 5, join with a sl st in first st. Cut yarn, leaving a long tail. (16 loops for sun rays)

Use tapestry needle to weave ends to middle of sun on WS. Use long tails to sew or tie motif to headband.

ASSEMBLY

Select the motif of your choice and position on the front left-hand side. Use any leftover yarn from crocheting the motif and sew the motif tightly in place.

Pastel Chevron Hat

Soft and gentle rainbows are created with an easy chevron stitch pattern. The Pastel Chevron Hat is worked flat and cinched closed at the top.

YOU WILL NEED

DK weight
60% cotton/40% acrylic
(153 yds/140 m, 1.75 oz/50 g)

* 1 ball of white (A)
* Small amounts in the
  following colors:
  rose pink (B), lilac (C),
  baby blue (D), mint green (E),
  lemon yellow (F)

EQUIPMENT

* US G-6 (4 mm) crochet hook
* Tapestry needle

GAUGE

16 sts and 8 rows = 4" (10 cm) in
chevron pattern

SIZE

Size: Newborn [0–3 months, 6–12
months]
Brim circumference: 13 [15, 17]"
(33 [38, 43] cm)
Length: 5½ [6, 6½]"
(14 [15, 16.5] cm), with brim folded

SPECIAL STITCHES

* Standing dc (see page 115)

TO MAKE

Brim

Foundation ch: With A, ch 10.
Row 1: Beg in second ch from hook,
work sc in back bump of each ch
across, ch 1, turn. (9 sts)
Row 2: Ch 1 (does not count as sc),
sc in first st, sc in back loop only of
next 8 sts, sc in last st, ch 1, turn.

Repeat row 2 until piece measures
13 [15, 17]" (33 [38, 43] cm).

Hat

Row 1 (RS): Rotate brim with one
long edge up, and yarn at right end
of work. Work 48 [56, 64] sc evenly
across. Fasten off, leaving an 8"
(20.5 cm) long tail for sewing. Do
not turn.

When adding each new color yarn for
the chevron section, be sure to leave a
6" (15 cm) tail of yarn to seam the hat.
Row 2 (RS): Join B with standing dc
in first st, work dc in base of same st,
dc in next st, (dc2tog) twice, dc in next
st. *2 dc in each of next 2 sts, dc in
next st, (dc2tog) twice, dc in next st;
repeat from * to last st. 2 dc in last st,
changing to C on last yo, turn.
(48 [56, 64] sts)
Row 3: With C, ch 3 (counts as dc),
work dc in base of same st as beg-ch.
dc in next st, (dc2tog) twice, dc in next
st, *2 dc in each of next 2 sts, dc in
next st, (dc2tog) twice, dc in next st;
repeat from * to last st. 2 dc in last st,
changing to D on last yo, turn.

Row 4: With D, repeat row 3, changing to E on last yo, turn.

Row 5: With E, repeat row 3, changing to F on last yo, turn.

Size Newborn only

Row 6: With F, repeat row 3, changing to A on last yo, turn.

Row 7: With A, repeat row 3.
Shape top.

Decrease row 1: Ch 3 (counts as dc), dc2tog, *dc in next st, dc2tog; repeat from * to end, turn. (32 sts remain)

Decrease row 2: Ch 3 (counts as dc), *dc2tog; repeat from * to last st, dc in last st, turn. (17 sts remain)

Decrease row 3: Ch 3 (counts as dc), *dc2tog; repeat from * to end. (9 sts remain) Fasten off, leaving a long tail for sewing.

Size 0–3 months only

Row 6: With F, repeat row 3, changing to B on last yo, turn.

Row 7: With B, repeat row 3, changing to A on last yo, turn.

Size 6–12 months only

Row 6: With F, repeat row 3, changing to B on last yo, turn.

Row 7: With B, repeat row 3, changing to C on last yo, turn.

Row 8: With C, repeat row 3, changing to A on last yo, turn.

Sizes 0–3 [6–12] months only
Shape top.

Decrease row 1: Ch 3 (counts as dc), dc2tog, *dc in next st, dc2tog; repeat from * to end, turn. (42 [48] sts remain)

Decrease row 2: Ch 3 (counts as dc), dc2tog, *dc in next st, dc2tog; repeat from * to end, turn. (28 [32] sts remain)

Decrease row 3: Ch 3 (counts as dc), *dc2tog; repeat from * to last st, dc in last st, turn. (15 [17] sts remain)

Decrease row 4: Ch 3 (counts as dc), *dc2tog; repeat from * to end. (8 [9] sts remain) Fasten off, leaving a long tail for sewing.

All sizes

FINISHING

Thread tail through remaining sts and pull tight to close top. Beginning at crown of hat and working to brim, seam the side edges of the hat closed; change colors for each section as you work. Weave in remaining ends.

To wear, fold half of brim up to RS.

Pastel Chevron Mittens

Flexible and lightweight, the simple drawstring closure allows you to gently secure the mittens to your baby's hands and protect them from their little nails.

YOU WILL NEED

DK weight
60% cotton/40% acrylic
(153 yds/140 m, 1.75 oz/50 g)

* 1 ball of white (A)
* Small amounts in the following colors: rose pink (B), lilac (C), baby blue (D), mint green (E), lemon yellow (F)

EQUIPMENT
* US G-6 (4 mm) crochet hook
* Tapestry needle

GAUGE
16 sts and 8 rows = 4" (10 cm) in chevron pattern

SIZE
Size: Newborn [3–6 months]
Hand circumference: 5 [6]"
(12.5 [15] cm)
Length: 4½ [5]" (11.5 [12.5] cm)

TO MAKE

Cuff

Foundation ch: With A, ch 6.
Row 1: Beg in second ch from hook work sc in back bump of each ch across, ch 1, turn. (5 sts)
Row 2: Sl st in first st, sl st in back loop only of next 3 sts, sl st in last st, ch 1, turn.
Row 3: Ch 1 (does not count as sc), sc in first st, sc in back loop only of next 3 sts, sc in last st, ch 1, turn.

Repeat rows 2 and 3 until piece measures 4 [5]" (10 [12.5] cm).

SPECIAL STITCHES
* Standing dc (see page 115)
* Standing sc (see page 114)

Mitt

Row 1 (RS): Turn cuff with one long edge up, and yarn at right end of work. Work 20 [24] sc evenly across. Fasten off, leaving an 8" (20.5 cm) long tail for sewing. Do not turn.
Row 2 (RS): Join B with standing dc in first st, work 0 [1] dc in base of same st, dc in next st, 2 [0] dc in next 1 [0] st, 1 [0] dc in next 1 [0] st, (dc2tog) twice, dc in next st, *2 dc in each of next 2 sts, dc in next st, (dc2tog) twice, dc in next st; repeat from * 0 [1] more time, 2 dc in next st, 1 [0] dc in next 2 [0] sts, changing to D [C] on last yo, turn. (20 [24] sts)

Row 3: With D [C], ch 3 (counts as dc), work 0 [1] dc in base of same st as beg-ch, dc in next st, 2 [0] dc in next 1 [0] st, 1 [0] dc in next 1 [0] st, (dc2tog) twice, dc in next st, *2 dc in next 2 sts, dc in next st, (dc2tog) twice, dc in next st; repeat from * 0 [1] more time, 2 dc in next st, 1 [0] dc in next 2 [0] sts, changing to E [D] on last yo, turn.

Row 4: With E [D], repeat row 3, changing to F [E] on last yo, turn.

Row 5: With F [E], repeat row 3. End size Newborn here, and change to F on last yo for size 3–6 months only, turn.

Size Newborn only

Dec row 1 (RS): Join A with standing sc in first st, sc in next st, sc2tog, *sc in next 2 sts, sc2tog; repeat from * to end, ch 1 turn. (15 st remain]

Dec row 2 (WS): Ch 1 (counts as sc), sc2tog, *sc in next st, sc2tog; repeat from * to end. Fasten off, leaving a long tail for sewing. (10 sts remain)

Size 3–6 months only

Row 6: With F, repeat row 3 and fasten off at end of row.
Shape top.

Dec row 1 (RS): Join A with standing sc, sc2tog, *sc in next st, sc2tog; repeat from * to end, ch 1, turn. (16 sts remain)

Dec row 2 (WS): Ch 1 (counts as sc), sc2tog, *sc in next st, sc2tog; repeat

from * to last st, sc in last st. Fasten off, leaving a long tail for sewing. (11 sts remain)

All sizes
Make second mitt in same way as first.

FINISHING
Thread tail through remaining sts and pull tight to close top. Beginning at tip of mittens and working to cuff, seam the side edges of the mittens closed; change colors for each section as you work. Weave in ends.

Wrist Ties (make 2)

With F, ch 60. Fasten off. Weave in ends.

Secure the center of tie at center back of mitt. Weave ends of tie through sts above cuff. Tie in a bow on front of mitt.

Gradient Floor Blanket

The swirl of colors that radiates from the blanket's center will provide a focal point to your baby's nursery! The blanket can be easily modified into any size and shape.

YOU WILL NEED

Worsted weight
100% wool
(220 yds/200 m, 3.5 oz/100 g)

* 4 balls of white (A)
* 1 ball in the following colors:
  red (B), orange (C),
  bright yellow (D),
  lemon yellow (E), lime green (F),
  apple green (G), cobalt (H),
  cornflower blue (I), fuchsia (J),
  baby pink (K), claret (L),
  cyan (M), heather (N)

EQUIPMENT

* US 7 (4.5mm) crochet hook

GAUGE

Each motif measures 2¾" (7 cm)
in diameter, without edging

SIZE
43 x 43" (110 x 110 cm)

SPECIAL STITCHES
* 4 dc popcorn stitch (see page 64)
* 5 dc popcorn stitch (see page 64)

TO MAKE

Motif

Start with a magic ring.
Round 1: Ch 3, PC-4, ch 2, *PC-5, ch 2; repeat from * 4 more times, join with a sl st to top of beg-ch. [6 popcorns, 6 ch-2 sp]
Round 2: Sl st to next ch-sp, (ch 3, PC-4, ch 1, PC-5, ch 3) in same ch-sp, *(PC-5, ch 1, PC-5, ch 3) in next ch-sp; repeat from * 4 more times, join with a sl st to top of beg-ch. Cut yarn and fasten ends. [12 popcorns, 6 ch-3 sp]

Make 163 motifs, 13 each of colors B, C, D, E, F, G, H, I, and M; 12 motifs each of colors L and N; and 11 motifs each of colors J and K.

Joining

Beginning with the first motif at the upper left, work your way down in columns. When a column is complete, work the next column on the right, beginning again at the top and work your way down. Place colors in 13 columns, alternating 13 rows of 12 motifs each and 12 rows of 13 motifs each, and a final row of 7 motifs as shown in the diagram on page 65.

First Motif

Join A in a ch-3 sp, (2 hdc, ch 2, 2 hdc) in ch-3 sp, *hdc in PC-5, hdc in ch-1 sp, hdc in PC-5, (3 hdc, ch 2, 2 hdc) in ch-3 sp; repeat from * 4 more times, hdc in PC-5, hdc in ch-1 sp, hdc in

PC-5, hdc in ch-3 sp, join with a sl st in first hdc. Fasten off.

Subsequent Motifs

The motifs are joined in the ch-2 sp at each corner. Join A in a ch-3 sp, (2 hdc, ch 1, sl st in ch-2 sp of motif to be joined into, ch 1, 2 hdc) in ch-3 sp, work to end of round as for first motif, joining additional corners as needed. Fasten off.

FINISHING

Weave in ends. Block to measurements, pinning out corners of outer motifs.

POPCORN STITCH

Ch2, in the next stitch make 4 dc. Pull up a loop and take hook out of your work. Insert hook from front to back into the second beg ch, straight into the loop you just pulled up. Tighten yarn to your hook, yarn over, and pull through loop and beg ch. This tightens the 4 dc at the top and makes it pop at the front. Of course you can make even larger popcorns by adding 1 or 2 dc. By going in with your hook from back to front, you'll create a popcorn that pops at the back of your work.

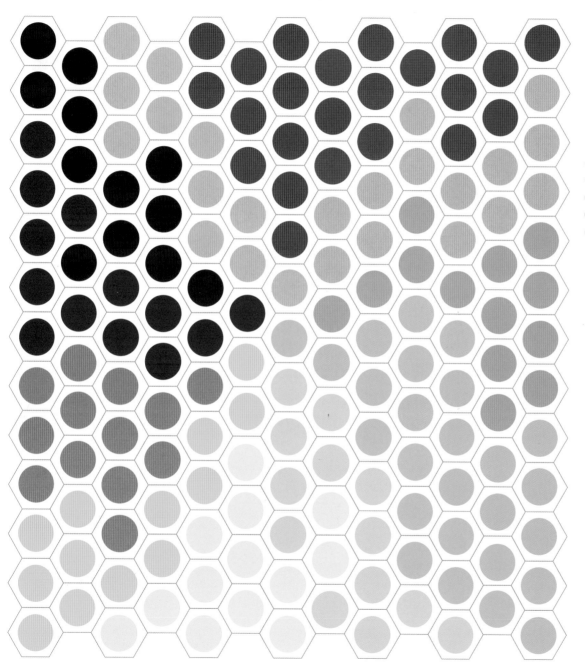

Key

- Claret (L), *12 motifs*
- Red (B), *13 motifs*
- Orange (C), *13 motifs*
- Bright yellow (D), *13 motifs*
- Lemon yellow (E), *13 motifs*
- Lime green (F), *13 motifs*
- Apple green (G), *13 motifs*
- Cyan (M), *13 motifs*
- Cobalt (H), *13 motifs*
- Cornflower blue (I), *13 motifs*
- Heather (N), *12 motifs*
- Fuchsia (J), *11 motifs*
- Baby pink (K), *11 motifs*

Pretty Mary Janes

The soft pastel colors used in this design make these shoes the perfect springtime gift. The little bows and buttons create adorable accents to this classic design.

YOU WILL NEED

Worsted weight
100% cotton
(82 yds/75 m, 1.75 oz/50 g)

* 1 ball in the following colors:
ecru (A), lilac (B)
* Small amounts in the
following colors:
sky blue (C), lime green (D),
pale yellow (E), apricot (F)

EQUIPMENT
* US G-6 (4 mm) crochet hook
* Tapestry needle
* Two ⅝" (15 mm) buttons

GAUGE
17 sts and 13 rows = 4" (10 cm) in
half double crochet

SIZE
Size: 0–6 months
Foot circumference: 4" (10 cm)
Foot length from heel:
3¼" (8 cm)

TO MAKE

Sole

Foundation ch: With A, ch 9.
Round 1: Work 3 dc in third ch from hook, 1 dc in each of next 5 ch, 7 dc in last chain, turn piece with remaining edge of foundation ch at top, 1 dc in each of next 5 ch, 3 dc in last ch, join with a sl st in first dc. (23 sts)
Round 2: Ch 2, 2 dc in next 3 sts, 1 dc in next 5 sts. 2 dc in each of next 7 sts, 1 dc in next 5 sts, dc in each of next 3 sts, join with a sl st in top of first dc. (36 sts)
   Fasten off.

Upper

Round 1: With B and RS facing, ch 1, work hdc in back loop only of each st around, join with a sl st in first hdc. (36 sts)
Round 2: Ch 1, sc around, join with a sl st in first sc.
Round 3: Ch 1, sc in next 10 sts, hdc2tog 3 times, hdc in next 4 sts, hdc2tog 3 times, sc to end, join with a sl st in first sc. (30 sts remain)
Round 4: Ch 1, sc in next 6 sts, hdc in next st, dc2tog 6 times, hdc into next st, sc to end, join with a sl st in first sc. (24 sts remain)
   Fasten off. Weave in all ends.

Straps (make 2)

Foundation ch: With B, ch 16.
Row 1: Beg in sixth ch from hook work hdc in next st to form button loop, then hdc to end. Fasten off, leaving a long tail for sewing.

Bow

Foundation ch: With B, ch 10.

Row 1: Beg in second ch from hook, hdc in each ch to end, change to C.

Row 2: Ch 2, turn, hdc in each st across, change to D.

Row 3: Ch 2, turn, hdc across, change to E.

Row 4: Ch 2, turn, hdc across, change to F.

Row 5: Ch 1, turn, hdc across, change to B.

Row 6: Ch 1, turn, hdc across. Fasten off.

FINISHING

Weave in all ends.

Sew one strap to each shoe, making sure straps are on opposite sides to each other. Sew a button to each shoe on opposite straps.

Pinch center of bow together using photo as a guide, sew a few sts around center of bow with B, then sew bow to shoe.

BOBBLE STITCH

With MC, insert hook in next st, yo and pull through a loop (2 loops on hook), drop MC and pick up CC, yo and pull through both loops on hook, working into same st just worked into (yo, insert hook in st and pull up a loop, yo and pull through 2 loops on hook) 5 times (6 loops on hook), drop CC and pick up MC, yo and pull through all loops on hook. (1 st remains on hook)

Bobble Pacifier Cords

Fun and function combined! These pacifier cords come together very quickly. So why limit yourself to only one when you can have a cord in every color?

YOU WILL NEED

Worsted weight
100% wool
(200 yds/200 m, 3.5 oz/100 g)

* 1 ball of white (MC)
* Small amount in the color of your choice (CC)

EQUIPMENT
* US 7 (4.5 mm) crochet hook
* Tapestry needle
* Fastener clip

GAUGE
16 sts = 4" (10 cm) in single crochet

SIZE
Width: 1¼ x 8¾" (3 x 22 cm)

TO MAKE

Cord

Foundation ch: With MC, ch 36.
Row 1: Beg in second ch from hook, sc in each ch across, ch 1, turn. (35 sts)
Row 2: Sc in each st across, ch 1, turn.
Row 3: 2 sc, *make bobble, 2 sc; repeat from * 10 more times, ch 1, turn. Cut CC.
Row 4: Repeat row 2.
Row 5: Sc in each st across, ch 1, rotate piece with end of rows at top edge, 1 sc in end of each row, ch 1, turn.
Row 6: Along end, sc2tog, sc, sc2tog. Cut yarn, leaving a long tail.

SPECIAL STITCH
* Bobble stitch (see page 68)

Loop
With MC, ch 25. Fasten off, leaving long tails at each end of ch.

FINISHING
Sew clip to shaped end of cord using long tail. Sew both ends of loop at other end of cord at row 3.

HANDY HINT

When working row 3, hold the contrasting color along the top of row 2 and work the single crochet with A over the top of the contrast color.

FOR THE NURSERY

Whatever the Weather Wall Hanging

This fun, colorful wall hanging will liven up any nursery! The bright, twirling 3-D shapes will be sure to excite and fascinate your little one.

YOU WILL NEED

Worsted weight
100% acrylic
(425 yds/389 m, 7 oz/197 g)

* Small amounts in the
following colors:
white (A), yellow (B), orange (C),
blue (D), green (E), red (F),
light blue (G), gold (H)

EQUIPMENT
* US G-6 (4.0 mm) crochet hook
* Fiberfill
* Stitch markers
* Tapestry needle
* Sewing needle
* Wooden mobile frame
* Super glue (optional)

GAUGE
Varies between motifs

SIZE
Cloud: 3 x 2½"
(7.75 x 6.5 cm)
Sun: 5 x 5" (13 x 13 cm)
Rainbow: 6½ x 3"
(17.5 x 7.75 cm)
Raindrop: 1 x 1½" (2.25 x 4 cm)
Star: 5 x 4" (13 x 10 cm)

SPECIAL STITCH
* Picot: ch3, sl st in 1st ch

TO MAKE

Cloud (make 2)

Round 1: Ch 1 in ring, work 8 sc in ring, do not join. Pull tail to close center. (8 sts)

Round 2: 2 sc in each st around, do not join. (16 sts)

Round 3: *Sc in next st, 2 sc in next st; repeat from * around, do not join. (24 sts)

Round 4: *Sc in next 2 sts, [2 hdc in next st, hdc in next 2 sts] twice, 2 sc in next st, sc in next 2 sts, 2 sc in next st; repeat from * once more, do not join. (32 sts)

Round 5: Sc in next 3 sts, 2 sc in next st, hdc in next 3 sts, 2 hdc in next st, hdc in next 2 sts, sc in next st, [2 sc in next st, sc in next 3 sts] twice, 2 hdc in next st, hdc in next 3 sts, 2 hdc in next st, sc in next 3 sts, 2 sc in next st, sc in next 3 sts, 2 sc in next st, do not join. (40 sts)

Rounds 6 and 7: Sc in each st around, do not join.

Round 8: Sc in next 3 sts, sc2tog, hdc in next 3 sts, hdc2tog, hdc in next 2 sts, sc in next st, sc2tog, sc in next 3 sts, sc2tog, sc in next 3 sts, hdc2tog, hdc in next 3 sts, hdc2tog, [sc in next 3 sts, sc2tog] twice, do not join. (32 sts remain)

Round 9: *Sc in next 2 sts, hdc2tog, hdc in next 2 sts, hdc2tog, hdc in next 2, sc2tog, sc in next 2 sts, sc2tog;

Sun (make 1)

Body

With B, make a magic ring.

Round 1: Ch 1 in ring, work 8 sc in ring, do not join. Pull tail to close center. (8 sts)

Round 2: 2 sc in each st around, do not join. (16 sts)

Round 3: *Sc in next st, 2 sc in next st; repeat from * around, do not join. (24 sts)

Round 4: *Sc in next 2 sts, 2 sc in next st; repeat from * around, do not join. (32 sts)

Round 5: *Sc in next 3 sts, 2 sc in next st; repeat from * around, do not join. (40 sts)

Rounds 6–11: Sc in each st around, do not join.

Round 12: *Sc in next 3 sts, sc2tog; repeat from * around, do not join. (32 sts remain)

Round 13: *Sc in next 2 sts, sc2tog; repeat from * around, do not join. (24 sts remain)

Round 14: *Sc in next st, sc2tog; repeat from * around, do not join. (16 sts remain)

Stuff sun tightly.

Round 15: [Sc2tog] around, do not join. (8 sts remain)

Cut yarn and weave the tail through the top of remaining sts, then pull tight to close hole. Weave in ends.

Sun Rays

Row 1 (RS): Beg in second ch from hook, *[sl st, sc] in next st, picot, [sc, sl st] in next st, sl st in next st, [sc, hdc] in next st, [dc, tr] in next st, picot, [tr, dc] in next st, [hdc, sc] in next st, sc in next st; repeat from * 4 more times, **[sc, hdc] in next st, [dc, tr] in next st, picot, [tr, dc] in next st, [hdc, sc] in next st, sl st in next st, [sl st, sc] in next st, picot, [sc, sl st] in next st, sl st in next st; repeat from ** 4 more times. (10 large rays and 10 small rays)

Cut yarn, leaving a long tail for sewing. Fold ray in half with WS together. Using the long tail, sew top edges tog, making sure rays match, sew the bottom together along foundation ch.

Sew rays to sun, centering them along the widest part, and with ends meeting. Weave in ends.

Rainbow (make 2)

Foundation ch: With D, ch 32, leaving a long tail, join with a sl st in first ch, being careful not to twist.

Round 1: Ch 1, *hdc in next 3 sts, 2 hdc in next st; repeat from * around. With E, join with a sl st in top of first hdc. Cut D. (40 sts)

Round 2: Ch 1, *hdc in next 4 sts, 2 hdc in next st; repeat from * around. With B, join with a sl st in top of first hdc. Cut E. (48 sts)

Round 3: Ch 1, *hdc in next 5 sts, 2

repeat from * once more, do not join. (24 sts remain)

Round 10: *Sc in next st, sc2tog; repeat from * around, do not join. (16 sts remain)

Round 11: [Sc2tog] around, do not join. (8 sts remain)

Stuff cloud, shaping the bumps in the cloud. Cut yarn and weave the tail through the top of remaining sts, then pull tight to close hole. Weave in ends.

hdc in next st; repeat from * around. With C, join with a sl st in top of first hdc. Cut B. (56 sts)

Round 4: Ch 1, *hdc in next 6 sts, 2 hdc in next st; repeat from * around. With F, join with a sl st in top of first hdc. Cut C. (64 sts)

Round 5: Ch 1, *hdc in next 7 sts, 2 hdc in next st; repeat from * around, join with a sl st in top of first hdc. Do not cut yarn. (72 sts)

Weave in ends, except for long tail of foundation ch. Fold ring in half to form an arch.

Using long tail from foundation ch, sew inner curve of arch closed.

With F, work sc together edges of outer curve, working through both sts. When about three-quarters of the edge has been joined, begin stuffing rainbow. Continue working sc to end and stuff as you go. Fasten off. Weave in ends.

Rain Drops (make 3)

Round 1: Ch 1 in ring, work 8 sc in ring, do not join. Pull tail tight to close center. (8 sts)

Round 2: 2 sc in each st around, do not join. (16 sts)

Rounds 3 and 4: Sc in each st around, do not join.

Round 5: *Sc in next 2 sts, sc2tog; repeat from * around, do not join. (12 sts remain)

Round 6: *Sc in next st, sc2tog; repeat from * around, do not join. (8 sts remain)

Stuff rain drop.

Round 7: [Sc2tog] around, do not join. (4 sts remain)

Cut yarn and weave the tail through the top of remaining sts, then pull tight to close hole. Weave in ends.

Star (make 2)

Front

With H, make a magic ring.

Round 1: Ch 1 in ring, work 5 sc in ring, join with a sl st in top of first sc. (5 sts)

Round 2: Ch 1, 2 sc in each st around, join with a sl st in top of first sc. (10 sts)

Round 3: Ch 1, sc in first st, [2 sc in next st, sc in next st] to last st, 2 sc in last st, join with a sl st in top of first sc. (15 sts)

Round 4: Ch 1, sc in first 2 sts, [2 sc in next st, sc in next 2 sts] to last 2 sts, 2 sc in last st, join with a sl st in top of first sc. (20 sts)

Place st markers in first, 5th, 9th, 13th, and 17th sts.

Row 1 (RS): Join H in first marked st with a sl st, ch 1, sc in next 4 sts, turn. (4 sts)

Row 2 (WS): Ch 1, sc2tog, sc in next 2 sts, turn. (3 sts remain)

Row 3: Ch 1, sc2tog, sc in next st, turn. (2 sts remain)

Row 4: Ch 1, sc2tog, fasten off.

Rep Rows 1–4 between marked sts 4 more times.

Next round: Join H in any st, ch 1, work 50 sc evenly around outer edge of star, join with a sl st in top of first sc. (50 sts)

Next round: Ch 1, sc in each st around, join with a sl st in top of first sc. Fasten off, leaving a long tail for sewing. Weave in ends.

Back

Make back in same way as front.

Using long tail, sew front and back together using the whip stitch, stuffing as you work. Fasten off. Weave in ends.

ASSEMBLY

Lay out a rain drop, cloud and rainbow for one strand, adjusting position until you are happy with each one. Cut a long strand of A and thread through each motif, knotting yarn at bottom and top of each motif to hold them into place. Repeat with two more rain drops, a cloud, and star, then with a star and a rainbow. Thread the sun on a short strand of yarn on its own.

Wrap each strand around the frame, adjusting length so each strand is a different length, and you achieve a fun, asymmetric effect. Secure the yarns tightly in place—add a small amount of super glue for extra security.

SKILL LEVEL

INTERMEDIATE

Climbing Colors Blanket

Bright colors climb a fluffy white background on this creative, reversible blanket. The combination of textures and colors will make this project a family favorite.

YOU WILL NEED

Worsted weight
100% acrylic
(247 yds/226 m, 4.5 oz/127 g)

* 4 balls of white (A)
* 1 ball in the following colors:
* red (B), orange (C), yellow (D), green (E), blue (F), purple (G)

EQUIPMENT
* US I-9 (5.5 mm) crochet hook
* Tapestry needle

GAUGE
13 sts and 7 rows = 4" (10 cm) in double crochet

* * * * * * * * * * * * * * * * * * * *

SIZE
31 x 43" (78.5 x 109 cm)

SPECIAL STITCH
* V-st: (see page 10).

STRIPE SEQUENCE
Working with A for every Part A, change contrasting colors every Part B in this order: *B, C, D, E, F, then G; repeat from * for stripe sequence.

* * * * * * * * * * * * * * * * * * * *

TO MAKE

Blanket

Foundation ch: With A, ch 98.
Row 1: Beg in second ch from hook, work sc in each ch across. (97 sts)
Row 2a: Ch 3 (counts as dc), dc in next st, ch 1, skip next 2 sts, 3 dc in next st, *ch1, skip next 3 sts, 3 dc in next st; repeat from * to last 4 sts, ch 1, skip next 2 sts, dc in last 2 sts.

(73 sts and 24 ch-sps)
Row 2b: Ch 1, turn, sc in first st, change to B, work around sts from previous row, ch 1, skip next st, V-st in skipped st below next ch, *ch 1, skip next 3 sts, V-st in skipped st below next ch; repeat from * to last 2 sts, ch 1, sl st in next st, skip last st. Fasten off B, but do not fasten off A.
(24 V-sts and 25 ch-sps)
Row 3a: Pick up A, work Stitch Pattern Part A.
Row 3b: With C, work Stitch Pattern Part B. Fasten off C, but not A.
   Repeat rows 3a and 3b, continuing in Stripe Sequence, work Part B with D, E, F, G, then repeat entire sequence 8 more times. Fasten off all colors.
   Weave in all ends.

Edging

Round 1: Do not turn. With A and top edge up, insert hook into first white st at beginning of previous row, yarn over and pull up a loop, ch 1, sc in same

(MULTIPLE OF 4 STS + 1)

Part A: Do not turn. With white (A), insert hook into first (white) st at beginning of previous row, yarn over and pull up a loop, ch 1, hdc in same st. Working into white sts from part A of the previous row, and around the colored stitches from part B, dc in next st, *ch 1, skip next V-st and next dc, 3 dc in next dc, skip next dc, repeat from * to last V-st, ch 1, skip next V-st, dc in last 2 sts.

Part B: Ch 1, turn, sc in first st and change to next contrasting color (B–G) according to Stripe Sequence. Working around white sts from part A, ch 1, skip next st, V-st in center of next V-st, *ch 1, skip next 3 sts, V-st in center of next V-st, repeat from * to last 2 sts, ch 1, sl st in next st, skip last st. Fasten off contrasting color, but not A.

st, hdc in next white st, *sc in center of next V-st, skip next white dc, 3 dc in next white dc, skip next white dc; repeat from * to last V-st, sc in center of last V-st, dc in last 2 white sts, rotate work with side edge at top, ch 1, work 135 sc evenly spaced across side edge, rotate work with foundation ch up, ch 1, sc in each ch across, rotate piece with remaining side edge up, ch 1, work 135 sc evenly spaced across side edge, join with a sl st in top of first sc.

(464 sts and 4 ch-sps)

Join with sl st to first st.

Round 2: Turn, [sl st, ch 1] in each st and ch-sp around, join with a sl st in first st. Fasten off. Weave in ends.

Mini Nesting Baskets

These nesting baskets are perfect for storing small items like cotton balls and hair bows. Make larger baskets by increasing the base and the sides by one round for each size.

YOU WILL NEED

Bulky weight
70% cotton/30% acrylic
(82 yds/75 m, 1.75 oz/50 g)

I ball in the following colors:
raspberry (A), coral (B), lemon (C),
turquoise (D)

EQUIPMENT

* US 7 (4.5 mm) crochet hook
* US H-8 (5 mm) crochet hook
* Stitch marker
* Tapestry needle

GAUGE

22 sts and 13 rounds = 4" (10 cm)
in half double crochet

SIZE

Small: 2½ x 2¼ x 2½"
(6.5 x 6 x 6.5 cm)
Medium: 3¼ x 2¾ x 3¼"
(8 x 7 x 8 cm)
Large: 3¾ x 3 x 3¾"
(9.5 x 7.5 x 9.5 cm)
Extra Large: 4½ x 3¼ x 4½"
(11.75 x 8 x 11.75 cm)

SPECIAL STITCHES

* FPsc (see page 112)

TURQUOISE BASKET

Base

With D and smaller crochet hook, make a magic ring, leaving a 4" (10 cm) long tail.

Round 1: Ch 2 (counts as hdc throughout), 9 hdc into ring, join with a sl st in top of beg-ch. (10 sts)

Round 2: Ch 2, hdc in st at base of beg-ch, 2 hdc in each st around, join with a sl st in top of beg-ch. (20 sts)

Round 3: Ch 2, hdc in st at base of beg-ch, hdc in next st, [2 hdc in next st, hdc in next st] 9 times, join with a sl st in top of beg-ch. (30 sts)

Round 4: Ch 2, hdc in st at base of beg-ch, hdc in next 2 sts, [2 hdc in next st, hdc in next 2 sts] 9 times, join with a sl st in top of beg-ch. (40 sts)

Round 5: Ch 2, hdc in st at base of beg-ch, hdc in next 3 sts, [2 hdc in next st, hdc in next 3 sts] 9 times, join with a sl st in top of beg-ch. (50 sts)

Round 6: Ch 2, hdc in st at base of beg-ch, hdc in next 4 sts, [2 hdc in next st, hdc in next 4 sts] 9 times, join with a sl st in top of beg-ch. (60 sts)

Round 7: Ch 2, hdc in st at base of beg-ch, hdc in next 5 sts, [2 hdc in next st, hdc in next 5 sts] 9 times, join with a sl st in top of beg-ch. Fasten off. (70 sts)

Sides

Change to larger crochet hook.

Round 1: Turn base with WS facing, join D with a FPsc around any st, FPsc in each st around, join with a sl st in first FPsc, mark the sl st, turn. (70 sts)

Round 2: Ch 1 (does not count as st throughout), sc in marked sl st, ch 1, skip next st, *sc in next st, ch 1, skip next st; rep from * around, join with a sl st in first sc. (35 sc and 35 ch-1 sp)

Round 3: Sl st in next ch-1 sp, [ch 1, sc, ch 1] in same ch-1 sp, [sc, ch 1] in each ch-1 sp around, join with a sl st in first sc. (35 sts and 35 ch-1 sp)

Rounds 4–12: Repeat round 3.

Round 13: Sl st into next ch-1 sp, ch 4 (counts as dc, ch 1), [dc, ch 1] in each ch-1 sp around, join with a sl st in third ch of beg-ch. (35 dc and 35 ch-1 sp)

Round 14: Ch 1, 2 sc in each ch-1 sp around, join with invisible join (see page 119). Fasten off. (70 sc)

YELLOW BASKET

Base

With C, work base in same way as for Turquoise Basket through round 6. Fasten off. (60 sts)

Sides

Change to larger crochet hook.

Round 1: Turn base with WS facing, join C with a FPsc around any st, FPsc in each st around, join with a sl st in first FPsc, mark the sl st, turn. (60 sts)

Rounds 2–11: Work in same way as for Turquoise Basket. (30 sc and 30 ch-1 sp)

Round 12: Sl st into next ch-1 sp, ch 4 (counts as dc, ch 1), [dc, ch 1] in each ch-1 sp around, join with a sl st in third ch of beg-ch. (30 dc and 30 ch-1 sp)

Round 13: Ch 1, 2 sc in each ch-1 sp around, join with invisible join. Fasten off. (60 sc)

ORANGE BASKET

Base

With B, work base in same way as for Turquoise Basket through round 5. Fasten off. (50 sts)

Sides

Change to larger crochet hook.

Round 1: Turn base with WS facing, join B with a FPsc around any st, FPsc in each st around, join with a sl st in first FPsc, mark the sl st, turn. (50 sts)

Rounds 2–10: Work in same way as for Turquoise Basket. (25 sc and 25 ch-1 sp)

Round 11: Sl st into next ch-1 sp, ch 4 (counts as dc, ch 1), [dc, ch 1] in each ch-1 sp around, join with a sl st in third ch of beg-ch. (25 dc and 25 ch-1 sp)

Round 12: Ch 1, 2 sc in each ch-1 sp around, join with invisible join. Fasten off. (50 sc)

RED BASKET

Base

With A, work base in same way as for Turquoise Basket through round 4. Fasten off. (40 sts)

Sides

Change to larger crochet hook.

Round 1: Turn base with WS facing, join A with a FPsc around any st, FPsc in each st around, join with a sl st in first FPsc, mark the sl st, turn. (40 sts)

Rounds 2–9: Work in same way as for Turquoise Basket. (20 sc and 20 ch-1 sp)

Round 10: Sl st into next ch-1 sp, ch 4 (counts as dc, ch 1), [dc, ch 1] in each ch-1 sp around, join with a sl st in third ch of beg-ch. (20 dc and 20 ch-1 sp)

Round 11: Ch 1, 2 sc in each ch-1 sp around, join with invisible join. Fasten off. (40 sc)

FINISHING

Weave in all ends.

Freddie Frog Bottle Cozy

Use a range of blue, purple, and green yarns to create a unique cozy
to cover your baby's milk bottle.

YOU WILL NEED

DK weight
60% cotton/40% acrylic
(153 yds/140 m, 1.75 oz/50 g)

* 1 ball in the following colors:
azure blue (A), lilac (B)
Small amounts in each of the
following colors:
lime green (C), grass green (D),
yellow (E), pink (F), white (G),
dark gray (H)

EQUIPMENT
* US E-4 (3.5 mm) crochet hook
* Stitch marker
* Tapestry needle

GAUGE
16 sts and 8 rows = 4" (10 cm) in
double crochet

SIZE

Fits 8" (20.5 cm) tall, 8 oz baby
bottle with straight or angled sides
(not curved)

TO MAKE

Bottle Cozy

Foundation ring: With A, ch 5, join
with a sl st in first ch to form a ring (or
make a magic ring).

Round 1: Ch 3 (counts as dc), 11 dc
in ring, join B and join last st with a sl
st in top of beg-ch; do not fasten off A
but leave at back of work. (12 sts)

Round 2: With B, ch 3 (counts as dc),
dc in same st, 2 dc in each st around,
pick up A and join with a sl st in top of
beg-ch, leave B at back of work.
(24 sts)

Round 3: With A, ch 3, dc in same st,
dc in next 5 sts, (2 dc in next st, dc in
next 5 sts) around, pick up B and join

with a sl st in top of beg-ch, leave A at
back of work. (28 sts)

Round 4: With B, ch 3, dc in next st
and in each st around, pick up A and
join with a sl st in top of beg-ch, leave
B at back of work.

Round 5: With A, ch 3, dc in next st
and in each st around, pick up B and
join with a sl st in top of beg-ch, leave
A at back of work.

Rounds 6–14: Repeat rounds 4 and 5
four times, then repeat round 4 once
more. Fasten off both colors.

APPLIQUÉS

Lily Pad

Foundation ch: With D, ch 16.

Row 1: Beg in fourth ch from hook,
work 4 dc in same st, dc in next 11 ch,
5 dc in last ch, rotate ch with opposite
side up, dc in next 11 ch, do not join.
Fasten off.

Flower

Foundation ring: With E, ch 5, join with a sl st in first ch to form a ring (or make a magic ring).

Round 1: Ch 1, 7 sc in ring, join with a sl st in first sc. Fasten off. (7 sts)

Round 2: Join F with a sl st in any sc, ch 1, 2 dc in same st, ch 1, (sl st in next sc, 2 dc in next st, ch 1) around, join with a sl st in first sl st. Fasten off. (7 petals)

Frog

Foundation ring: With C, ch 5, join with a sl st in first ch to form a ring (or make a magic ring).

Round 1: Ch 1, 8 sc in ring, do not join; work rounds in a spiral, place marker to mark beg of rounds. (8 sts)

Round 2: 2 sc in each st around. (16 sts)

Round 3: (2 sc in next st, sc in next st) around. (24 sts)

Round 4: Skip next st, 7 tr in next st, skip next st, sc in next st, skip next st, 7 tr in next st, skip next st, sc in next 3 sts, (3 tr, ch 4, sl st) in next st, sc in next 9 sts, (sl st, ch 4, 3 tr) in next st, sc in next 2 sts, sl st in next st. Fasten off.

Eyes (make 2)

Round 1: With H, ch 2, work 6 sc in second ch from hook, join with a sl st in first sc. Fasten off. (6 sts)

Round 2: Join G with sc in any st, sc in same st, 2 sc in each st around, join with a sl st in first sc. Fasten off. (12 sts)

Sew eyes to 7-tr shells at top of frog, with green showing around eyes as shown in photo.

FINISHING

Weave in ends on all pieces.

Bottle Cozy Drawstring

With D, ch 50. Fasten off, leaving a small tail.

Thread drawstring through stitches of last round of cozy.

Cut 4 pieces of D, each 4" (10 cm) long for tassels. Holding 2 pieces together, fold in half and pull loop through end st of chain, then pull all ends through loop. Pull snug and trim all ends to 1" (2.5 cm). Repeat with remaining 2 pieces of D on other end of chain. Tie bow snugly around neck of bottle.

Sew lily pad to bottle cozy, then frog on top of lily pad, using photo as reference. Sew flower to bottle cozy, sewing around center and leaving petals free. Slip cozy over bottle.

Monster Pillow Cover

Creative and easy to make, this Monster Pillow Cover can also be used to store toys and baby clothes. The simple back flap makes it easy to remove the pillow for cleaning.

YOU WILL NEED

Bulky weight
70% cotton/30% acrylic
(82 yds/75 m, 1.75 oz/50 g)

* 2 balls of sky blue (A)
* 1 ball in the following colors:
grass green (B), coral (C),
lemon yellow (D), white (E)

EQUIPMENT

* US 7 (4.5 mm) crochet hook
* Stitch marker
* Two small circles of felt in black
or dark brown
* Embroidery thread in black or
dark brown
* Tapestry needle

GAUGE

13½ sts and 10 rows = 4" (10 cm)
in pattern

● ●
SIZE
11¾ x 15¾" (30 x 40 cm)

● ●

TO MAKE

Ears (make 1 in C and 1 in D)

Round 1: Make a magic ring, ch 1, 6 sc into ring, do not join. (6 sts)

Round 2: 2 sc in each st around, do not join. (12 sts)

Round 3: *Sc in next st, 2 sc in next st; repeat from * 5 more times, do not join. (18 sts)

Rounds 4–7: Sc in each st around, sl st in next st of last round. Fasten off. Weave in ends.

Legs (make 2)

Round 1: With A, make a magic ring, ch 1 (does not count as a st), 6 sc into ring, do not join. (6 sts)

Round 2: 2 sc in each st around, do not join. (12 sts)

Round 3: *Sc in next st, 2 sc in next st; repeat from * 5 more times, do not join. (18 sts)

Rounds 4–13: Sc in each st around, sl st in next st of last round. Fasten off. Weave in ends.

Body

Body begins at the top of the back and works down to the bottom when the legs are joined. Work then continues up the front, when the ears are joined on the last row of the front.

Foundation ch: With E, ch 41.

Row 1 (WS): Beg in second ch from hook, sc in each ch to end, turn. (40 sts)

Row 2 (RS): Ch 2 (does not count as a st), dc in each st to end, turn.

Row 3: Ch 1 (does not count as st), sc in each st to the end, turn.

Row 4: Repeat row 2, changing to B at end of row.

Rows 5–8: With B, work in established patt, changing to D at end of last row.

Rows 9–12: With D, work in

etablished patt, changing to C at end of last row.

Rows 13–16: With C, work in established patt, changing to E at end of last row.

Rows 17–20: With E, work in established patt, changing to B at end of last row.

Rows 21–24: With B, work in established patt, changing to D at end of last row.

Rows 25–28: With D, work in established patt, changing to C at end of last row.

Row 29: With C, ch 1, sc in first 5 sts, holding first leg behind body and with top edges held together, work sc in next 9 sts, working through all 3 layers, sc in next 12 sts, hold second leg behind body same as first leg and sc in next 9 sts same as first leg, sc to end, turn.

Rows 30–32: With C, work in established patt, changing to E at end of last row.

Rows 33–36: With E, work in established patt, changing to B at end of last row.

Rows 37–40: With B, work in established patt, changing to D at end of last row.

Rows 41–44: With D, work in established patt, changing to C at end of last row.

Rows 45–48: With C, work in established patt, changing to A at end

of last row.

Rows 49–68: With A, work in established patt.

Row 69: With A, ch 1, holding first ear behind body and with top edges held together, work sc in first 9 sts working through all 3 layers, sc in next 22 sts, hold second ear behind body same as first ear and sc in next 9 sts same as first ear, turn.

Rows 70–89: With A, work in established patt. Fasten off.

Weave in all ends.

Big Eye (make 1)

Foundation: With E, make a magic ring.

Round 1: Ch 1 (does not count as a st), 6 sc into ring, do not join. (6 sts)

Round 2: 2 sc in each st around, do not join. (12 sts)

Round 3: *Sc in next st, 2 sc in next st; repeat from * 5 more times, do not join. (18 sts)

Round 4: *2 sc in next st, sc in each of next 2 sts; repeat from * 5 more times, do not join. (24 sts)

Round 5: *Sc in each of next 3 sts, 2 sc in next st; repeat from * 5 more times, do not join. (30 sts)

Round 6: *Sc in next st, 2 sc in next st, sc in each of next 3 sts; repeat from * 5 more times, do not join. (36 sts)

Round 7: *Sc in each of next 3 sts, 2 sc in next st, sc in each of next 2 sts;

repeat from * 5 more times, join with a sl st in next st. Fasten off. (42 sts)

Small Eye (make 1)

Rounds 1–5: Make in same way as for Big Eye, sl st in next st at end of last round. Fasten off. (30 sts)

Arms (make 1 in B and 1 in D)

Foundation: Make a magic ring.

Round 1: Ch 1 (does not count as a st), 6 sc into ring, do not join. (6 sts)

Round 2: 2 sc in each st around, do not join. (12 sts)

Rounds 3–7: Sc in each st around, do not join.

Round 8: *Sc in next st, sc2tog; repeat from * 3 more times, do no join. (8 sts remain)

Rounds 9–20: Sc in each st around, join with a sl st in next st of last round. Fasten off. Weave in ends.

FINISHING

Pin eyes to front of head, and with B threaded in tapestry needle, sew eyes to head using running st.

Sew circles of felt onto each eye using blanket stitch. Embroider mouth with C. Fold body at rows 29 and 69 with RS on outside, and top of back overlapping the lower part.

With C, join each side edge by working a row of sc through all layers. Fasten off. Sew arms to sides of body.

Fun-shapes Organizer

Whether it's toys or toiletries, this organizer is a great place to keep all of your baby's belongings—and it brightens up the nursery!

YOU WILL NEED

Worsted weight
100% cotton
(87 yds/80 m, 1.75 oz/50 g)

* 4 balls of turquoise (A)
* I ball in the following colors:
lime green (B), orange (C), red (D),
light gray (E), bright yellow (F)

EQUIPMENT

* US H-8 (5 mm) crochet hook
* Stitch marker
* Three 1" (25 mm) buttons
* Hanger measuring about 15"
(38 cm) across bottom

GAUGE

15 sts and 17 rows = 4" (10 cm) in
single crochet

SIZE

14¾ x 17½" (37.5 x 44.5 cm), with
top folded over.

TO MAKE

Main Panel

Foundation ch: With A, ch 56.
Row 1: Beg in sc in second ch from hook, sc in each ch across, turn. (55 sts)
Row 2: Ch 1, sc in each sc across, turn.

Repeat last row until piece measures approximately 17¾" (45 cm).
Buttonhole row: Ch 1, sc in first 8 sts, (ch 3, skip next 3 sts, sc in next 15 sts) 2 times, ch 3, skip next 3 sts, sc in last 8 sts, turn.

Repeat row 2 three more times.
Fasten off. Weave in ends.

Top Pockets

Foundation ch: With C, ch 17.
Row 1: Beg in second ch from hook, sc in each ch across, turn. (16 sts)
Row 2: Ch 1, sc in each st across, turn.
Rows 3–18: Repeat row 2, then fasten off at end of last row.
Row 19: Join B with sc in first st, sc in each st across, turn.
Rows 20–40: Repeat row 2, then fasten off at end of last row.
Row 41: Join D with sc in first st, sc in each st across, turn.
Rows 42–58: Repeat row 2, then fasten off at end of last row.
Weave in ends.

Bottom Pockets

Foundation ch: With E, ch 24.
Row 1: Beg in sc in second ch from hook and sc in each ch across, turn. (23 sts)
Row 2: Ch 1, sc in each st across, turn.
Rows 3–18: Repeat row 2, then fasten

off at end of last row.

Row 19: Join F with sc in first st, sc in each st across, turn.

Rows 20–40: Repeat row 2, then fasten off at end of last row.

Row 41: Join B with sc in first st, sc in each st across, turn.

Rows 42–58: Repeat row 2, then fasten off at end of last row.

Weave in ends.

Geometric Pieces

Circle (make 1 in D and 1 in E)

Foundation round: Ch 5, join with a sl st in first ch to form ring (or make a magic ring).

Round 1: Ch 1, 8 sc in ring, do not join; work rounds in a spiral, place marker to mark beginning of round. (8 sts)

Round 2: 2 sc in each st around. (16 sts)

Round 3: (2 sc in next st, sc in next st) around, join with a sl st in next st. (24 sts)

Fasten off, leaving a long tail for sewing.

Long Vertical Rectangle (make 1 in F and 1 in B)

Foundation ch: Ch 7.

Row 1: Beg in second ch from hook, sc in each ch across, turn. (6 sts)

Row 2: Ch 1, sc in each st across, turn.

Rows 3–12: Repeat row 2, then fasten off at end of last row, leaving a long tail for sewing.

Small Square (make 1 in D)
Foundation ch: Ch 7.

Row 1: Beg in second ch from hook and sc in each ch across, turn. (6 sts)

Row 2: Ch 1, sc in each st across, turn.

Rows 3–6: Repeat row 2, then fasten off at end of last row, leaving a long tail for sewing.

Medium Square (make 2 in C)
Foundation ch: Ch 9.

Row 1: Beg in second ch from hook and sc in each ch across, turn. (8 sts)

Row 2: Ch 1, sc in each st across, turn.

Rows 3–8: Repeat row 2, then fasten off at end of last row, leaving a long tail for sewing.

Large Square (make 1 in A)
Foundation ch: Ch 11.

Row 1: Beg in second ch from hook and sc in each ch across, turn. (10 sts)

Row 2: Ch 1, sc in each st across, turn.

Rows 3–10: Repeat row 2, then fasten off at end of last row, leaving a long tail for sewing.

Long Horizontal Rectangle (make 1 in A)
Foundation ch: Ch 13.

Row 1: Beg in second ch from hook and sc in each ch across, turn. (12 sts)

Row 2: Ch 1, sc in each st across, turn.

Rows 3–6: Repeat row 2, then fasten off at end of last row, leaving a long tail for sewing.

Small Vertical Rectangle (make 1 in E)
Foundation row: Ch 5.

Row 1: Beg in second ch from hook and sc in each ch across, turn. (4 sts)

Row 2: Ch 1, sc in each st across, turn.

Rows 3–8: Repeat row 2, then fasten off at end of last row, leaving a long tail for sewing.

FINISHING
Weave in beginning tails of each geometric piece.

Block main panel to 14¾" (37.5 cm) *wide and 18¾" (47.5 cm) long, top pocket to 4¼" (11 cm) wide and 13¾" (35 cm) long, and bottom pocket to 6¼" (16 cm) wide and 13¾" (35 cm) long (see page 121).

Place each geometric piece on both pockets, using photo as a guide. Sew each piece to pocket using the long tails.

Pin both pockets to main panel as shown in photo. With D and RS facing, begin at top of bottom pocket, join pocket to main panel with sl st through both layers along sides and bottom, then continuing sl st around remaining edges, joining sides of top pocket as you work. Fasten off.

With D and RS facing, join bottom edge of top pocket using sl st along bottom edge. Fasten off.

With D and RS facing, sl st along color divisions of each pocket to form smaller pockets. Fasten off at end of each pocket seam.

Sew buttons to RS, 15 rows from top edge. Button top edge over hanger.

Drops Storage Basket

Form meets function in this sturdy storage basket. The top can be rolled down for added stability, or use the handles for easy, one-handed carry.

YOU WILL NEED

Bulky weight
100% acrylic
(114 yds/132 m, 7.76 oz/220 g)

* 3 balls of light blue (A)
* 1 ball of charcoal (B)
* Small amounts in the
following colors:
red (C), yellow (D), green (E),
blue (F), purple (G)

EQUIPMENT
* US N/P-15 (10 mm) crochet
hook
* Tapestry needle

GAUGE
7 sts and 6 rows = 4" (10 cm) in
double crochet

SIZE
11¾ × 11¾ × 11¾"
(30 x 30 x 30 cm)

SPECIAL STITCHES
* FPtr (see page 112)
* BPhdc (see page 112)

TO MAKE

Base

Foundation ring: With 2 strands of B held together, make a magic ring, leaving a 4" (10 cm) tail.

Round 1: Ch 3 (counts as dc), dc, tr, (2 dc, tr) 3 times, join with a sl st in top of beg-ch, sl st in next dc and tr. (12 sts)

Round 2: Ch 3 (counts as dc throughout), (dc, tr, 2 dc) in st at base of beg-ch, dc in next 2 sts, *(2 dc, tr, 2 dc) in next st, dc in next 2 sts; rep from * around, join with a sl st in top of beg-

ch, sl st in next dc and tr. (28 sts)

Round 3: Ch 3, (dc, tr, 2 dc) in st at base of beg-ch, dc in next 6 sts, *(2 dc, tr, 2 dc) in next st, dc in next 6 sts; rep from * around, join with a sl st in top of beg-ch, sl st in next dc and tr. (44 sts)

Round 4: Ch 3, (dc, tr, 2 dc) in st at base of beg-ch, dc in next 10 sts, * (2 dc, tr, 2 dc) in next st, dc in next 10 sts; rep from * around, join with a sl st in top of beg-ch, sl st in next dc and tr. (60 sts)

Round 5: Ch 3, (dc, tr, 2 dc) in st at base of beg-ch, dc in next 14 sts, * (2 dc, tr, 2 dc) in next st, dc in next 14 sts; rep from * around, join with a sl st in top of beg-ch, sl st in next dc and tr. (76 sts)

Round 6: Ch 3, (dc, tr, 2 dc) in st at base of beg-ch, dc in next 18 sts, * (2 dc, tr, 2 dc) in next st, dc in next 18 sts; rep from * around, join with a sl st in top of beg-ch. (92 sts)

Fasten off. Weave in ends.

Sides

Round 1: With 2 strands of A held together and RS facing, join yarn with a sl st around the back post of any corner tr, ch 2 (counts as hdc throughout), BPhdc in each st around, join with a sl st in top of beg-ch. (92 sts)

Round 2: Sl st in next 2 sts, ch 2, hdc in next 20 sts, skip next 2 sts, *hdc in next 21 sts, skip next 2 sts; rep from * 2 more times, join with a sl st in top of beg-ch. (84 sts remain)

Round 3: Sl st in next st, ch 2, hdc in next 19 sts, FPtr around first skipped st from round 1, skip next st of round 2, *hdc in next 20 st, FPtr around first skipped st from round 1, skip next st of round 2; rep from * 2 more times, join with a sl st in top of beg-ch. (84 st)

Round 4: Ch 2, hdc in each st around, join with a sl st in top of beg-ch.

Round 5: Sl st in next st, ch 2, hdc in next 19 sts, FPtr around FPtr 2 rounds below, skip next st of previous round, *hdc in next 20 sts, FPtr around FPtr 2 rounds below, skip next st of previous round; rep from * 2 more times, join with a sl st in top of beg-ch.

Rounds 6–13: Repeat rounds 4 and 5 four more times.

Round 14: Repeat round 4.

Round 15: Sl st in next st, ch 2, hdc in next 6 sts, ch 6, skip next 6 sts, hdc in next 7 sts, FPtr around FPtr 2 rounds below, skip next st of previous round, hdc in next 20 sts, FPtr around FPtr 2 rounds below, skip next st of previous round, hdc in next 7 sts, ch 6, skip next 6 sts, hdc in next 7 sts, FPtr around FPtr 2 rounds below, skip next st of previous round, hdc in next 20 sts, FPtr around FPtr 2 rounds below, skip next st of previous round, join with a sl st in top of beg-ch. (72 sts and 2 ch-6 sp)

Round 16: Ch 2, hdc in next 6 sts, 6 hdc in ch-6 sp, hdc in next 36 sts, 6 hdc in ch-6 sp, hdc in next 29 sts, join with a sl st in top of beg-ch. (84 sts)

Round 17: Repeat round 5. Fasten off.

FINISHING

Weave in ends.

Rainbow Waves Stroller Blanket

This beautiful rainbow blanket, with its front post stitches, will keep your little one cozy and protected from the cold.

YOU WILL NEED

Worsted weight
50% merino wool/25% acrylic/
25% microfiber
(115 yds/105 m, 1.75 oz/50 g)

2 balls of orange (G), yellow (H)
∗ 1 ball in the following colors:
purple (A), off-white (B), red (C),
turquoise (D), bright green (E),
cyan (F)

EQUIPMENT

∗ US G-6 (4 mm) crochet hook
∗ Stitch marker
∗ Tapestry needle

GAUGE

18 sts and 19 rows = 4" (10 cm) in
alternating rows of single crochet
and half double crochet

SIZE

28 x 24" (71 x 61 cm)

SPECIAL STITCHES

FPtr (see page 112)

STRIPE SEQUENCE

10 rows with A, 1 row with B, 11
rows with C, 1 row with B, 13
rows with D, 1 row with B, 13
rows with E, 1 row with B, 2 rows
with A, 13 rows with F, 1 row with
B, 17 rows with G, 1 row with B, 2
rows with C, 9 rows with H, 1 row
with B, 7 rows with G, 1 row with
B, then 10 rows with H.

WORKING THE LOOPS

All single crochets (sc) used in the
main blanket pattern are worked
under 3 loops of hdc.

TO MAKE

Foundation ch: With A, ch 126.

Row 1 (WS): Beg in third ch from hook (skipped ch do not count as a st), hdc in each ch across, turn. (124 sts)

Row 2 (RS): Ch 1 (does not count as a st), sc in first 4 sts, *FPtr in same st as last sc, skip next st in previous row, sc in next 5 sts, FPtr around last st of previous row worked, FPtr around next st in previous row (the st below last FPtr), skip 2 sts in previous row behind the 2 FPtr, sc in next 7 sts; rep from * 7 more times, turn.

Row 3 (WS): Ch 2 (does not count as a st), hdc in each st across, turn.

Row 4: Ch 1, sc in first 5 sts, *FPtr around FPtr 2 rows below, skip next st of previous row, sc in next 5 sts, FPtr around each of 2 FPtr 2 rows below, skip 2 sts in previous row**, sc in next 7 sts; rep from * 6 more times, then from * to ** once, sc in last 6 sts, turn.

Row 5: Repeat row 3.

Row 6: Ch 1, sc in first 6 sts, *FPtr

around FPtr 2 rows below, skip next st of previous row, sc in next 5 sts, FPtr around each of 2 FPtr 2 rows below, skip next 2 sts of previous row**, sc into next 7 sts; rep from * 6 more times, then rep from * to ** once, sc in last 5 sts, turn.

Row 7: Repeat row 3.

Row 8: Ch 1, sc in first 7 sts, *FPtr around FPtr 2 rows below, skip next st of previous row, sc in next 5 sts, FPtr around each of 2 FPtr 2 rows below, skip next 2 sts of previous row**, sc in next 7 sts; rep from * 6 more times, then from * to ** once, sc in last 4 sts, turn.

Row 9: Repeat row 3.

Row 10: Repeat row 8.

Row 11: With B, repeat row 3.

Row 12: With C, repeat row 6.

Row 13: Repeat row 3.

Row 14: Repeat row 4.

Row 15: Repeat row 3.

Row 16: Ch 1, sc in first 4 sts, *FPtr around FPtr 2 rows below, skip next st of previous row, sc in next 5 sts, FPtr around each of 2 FPtr from 2 rows below, skip next 2 sts of previous row, sc in next 7 sts; rep from * 7 more times, turn.

Row 17: Repeat row 3.

Row 18: Repeat row 16.

Row 19: Repeat row 3.

Rows 20–115: Repeat rows 4–19 six more times, working colors in established Stripe Sequence. Do not fasten off after last row, turn.

Edging

Round 1: With RS facing, ch 1, 3 sc in first st, sc in next 122 sts, 3 sc in last st to turn corner, 115 sc evenly spaced along side edge (1 sc in each row), 3 sc in first ch of foundation ch to turn corner, sc in next 122 ch, 3 sc in last ch to turn corner, 115 sc evenly spaced along remaining side edge, join with a sl st in first sc. Fasten off.

Round 2 (RS): Join B with a sl st in any st along edge, ch 1, working from left to right, *insert hook in st to right of hook, yo and draw through a loop, yo and draw through both loops on hook; repeat from * around, join with a sl st in top of first reverse sc. Fasten off.

FINISHING

Weave in all ends and block.

COLOR CHANGE

When changing colors for the next row, work the last yarn over of the last stitch of the row with the new color for a smooth transition.

Buddy Bear Curtain Tie

This little bear will brighten up any nursery! Use fun colors to complement
or contrast with your room design.

YOU WILL NEED

DK weight
50% cotton/50% polyester
(115 yds/105 m, 1.75 oz/50 g)

* 1 ball in the following colors:
pale lilac (A), light purple (B),
bright pink (C), light pink (D),
cream (E), bright purple (F)

EQUIPMENT
* US D-3 (3.25 mm) crochet hook
* 2 × small safety eyes
* 1 × ¾" (15 mm) button
* Fiberfill

GAUGE
24 sts and 24 rounds = 4" (10 cm)
in single crochet

SIZE
Head circumference: 9" (23 cm)
Length: 7" (18 cm)

TO MAKE

Head

With A, make a magic ring.

Round 1: Ch 1 in ring, work 6 sc in ring, join with a sl st in top of first sc. (6 sts)

Round 2: Ch 1, 2 sc in each st around, join with a sl st in top of first sc. Fasten off A. (12 sts)

Round 3: Join B with a sl st, ch 1, sc in first st, [2 sc in next st, sc in next st] to last st, 2 sc in last st, join with a sl st in top of first sc. (18 sts)

Round 4: Ch 1, sc in first 2 sts, [2 sc in next st, sc in next 2 sts] to last st, 2 sc in last st, join with a sl st in top of first sc. Fasten off. (24 sts)

Round 5: Join C with a sl st, ch 1, sc in first 3 sts, [2 sc in next st, sc in next 3 sts] to last st, 2 sc in last st, join with a sl st in top of first sc. (30 sts)

Round 6: Ch 1, sc in first 4 sts, [2 sc in next st, sc in next 4 sts] to last st, 2 sc in last st, join with a sl st in top of first sc. Fasten off C. (36 sts)

Round 7: Join D with a sl st, ch 1, sc in first 5 sts, [2 sc in next st, sc in next 5 sts] to last st, 2 sc in last st, join with a sl st in top of first sc. (42 sts)

Round 8: Ch 1, sc in first 6 sts, [2 sc in next st, sc in next 6 sts] to last st, 2 sc in last st, join with a sl st in top of first sc. Fasten off D. (48 sts)

Round 9: Join E with a sl st, ch 1, sc in first 7 sts, [2 sc in next st, sc in next 7 sts] to last st, join with a sl st in top of first sc. (54 sts)

Round 10: Ch 1, sc in each st around, join with a sl st in top of first sc. Fasten off E.

Rounds 11 and 12: Join F with a sl st, ch 1, sc in each st around, join with a sl st in top of first sc. Fasten off at end of round 12.

Round 13: Join A with a sl st, ch 1, sc in each st around, join with a sl st in top of first sc.

Round 14: Ch 1, sc in first 22 sts, ch 1, skip next st, sc in next 9 sts, ch 1, skip next st, sc in each st to end of round, join with a sl st in top of first sc. Fasten off A.

Round 15: Join B with a sl st, ch 1, sc in each st and ch-sp around, join with a sl st in top of first sc.

Round 16: Ch 1, sc in each st around, join with a sl st in top of first sc. Fasten off B.

Rounds 17 and 18: Join C with a sl st, ch 1, sc in each st around, join with a sl st in top of first sc. Fasten off at end of round 18.

Round 19: Join D with a sl st, ch 1, sc in first 7 sts, [sc2tog, sc in next 7 sts] to last 2 sts, sc2tog, join with a sl st in top of first sc. (48 sts remain)

Round 20: Ch 1, sc in first 6 sts, [sc2tog, sc in next 6 sts] to last 2 sts, sc2tog, join with a sl st in top of first sc. Fasten off D. (42 sts remain)

Round 21: Join E with a sl st, ch 1, sc in first 5 sts, [sc2tog, sc in next 5 sts] to last 2 sts, sc2tog, join with a sl st in top of first sc. (36 sts remain)

Round 22: Ch 1, sc in first 4 sts, [sc2tog, sc in next 4 sts] to last 2 sts, sc2tog, join with a sl st in top of first sc.

Fasten off E. (30 sts remain)

Insert eyes into holes in Round 14 following manufacturer's instructions. Beg stuffing head now, and add additional fiberfill as you work.

Round 23: Join F with a sl st, ch 1, sc in first 3 sts, [sc2tog, sc in next 3 sts] to last 2 sts, sc2tog, join with a sl st in top of first sc. (24 sts remain)

Round 24: Ch 1, sc in first 2 sts, [sc2tog, sc in next 2 sts] to last 2 sts, sc2tog, join with a sl st in top of first sc. Fasten off F. (18 sts remain)

Round 25: Join A with a sl st, ch 1, sc in first st, [sc2tog, sc in next st] to last 2 sts, sc2tog, join with a sl st in top of first sc. (12 sts remain)

Round 26: Ch 1, [sc2tog] around, join with a sl st in top of first st. Fasten off A, leaving a long tail. (6 sts remain)

Thread tail through tops of remaining sts, then pull tight to close hole. Fasten off.

Muzzle

Foundation ch: With A, ch 3.

Round 1: Beg in second ch from hook, work 5 sc in each of next 2 ch, join with a sl st in top of first sc. (10 sts)

Round 2: Ch 1, sc in first 2 sts, 2 sc in each of next 3 sts, sc in next 2 sts, 2 sc in next 3 sts, join with a sl st in top of first sc. (16 sts)

Round 3: Ch 1, sc in first 5 sts, 2 sc in next st, sc in next 7 sts, 2 sc in next st, sc in next 2 sts, join with a sl st in top of first sc. (18 sts)

Round 4: Ch 1, sc in first 5 sts, 2 sc in each of next 2 sts, sc in next 7 sts, 2 sc in each of next 2 sts, sc in next 2 sts, join with a sl st in top of sc. (20 sts)

Fasten off, leaving a tail for sewing. Begin sewing muzzle to head as shown in photo and lightly fill with fiberfill as you work. Embroider nose and mouth with F, using straight and satin sts.

Body

With A, make a magic ring.

Rounds 1–7: Work same as for head. (42 sts)

Round 8: Ch 1, sc in each st around, join with a sl st in top of first sc. Fasten off D.

Rounds 9 and 10: Join E with a sl st, ch 1, sc in each st around, join with a sl st in top of first sc. Fasten off E at end of round 10.

Round 11: Join F with a sl st, ch 1, sc in first 5 sts, [sc2tog, sc in next 5 sts] to last 2 sts, sc2tog, join with a sl st in top of first sc. (36 sts remain)

Round 12: Ch 1, sc in each st around, join with a sl st in top of first sc. Fasten off F.

Round 13: Join A with a sl st, ch 1, sc in first 4 sts, [sc2tog, sc in next 4 sts] to last 2 sts, sc2tog, join with a sl st in top of first sc. (30 sts remain)

Round 14: Ch 1, sc in each st around, join with a sl st in top of first sc. Fasten off A.

Rounds 15 and 16: Join B with a sl st, ch 1, sc in each st around, join with a sl st in top of first sc. Fasten off B at end of round 16. Beg stuffing head now, and add additional fiberfill as you work.

Round 17: Join C with a sl st, ch 1, sc in first 3 sts, [sc2tog, sc in next 3 sts] to last 2 sts, sc2tog, join with a sl st in top of first sc. (24 sts remain)

Round 18: Ch 1, sc in first 2 sts, [sc2tog, sc in next 2 sts] to last 2 sts, sc2tog, join with a sl st in top of first sc. Fasten off C. (18 sts remain)

Round 19: Join D with a sl st, ch 1, sc in first st, [sc2tog, sc in next st] to last 2 sts sc2tog, join with a sl st in top of first sc. Fasten off D, leaving a long tail. (12 sts remain)

Complete stuffing body then sew it to head.

Ears (make 2)

With A, make a magic ring.

Row 1: Ch 1 in ring, work 6 dc in ring, ch 1 and turn. Do not join (6 sts)

Row 2: Sc in first st, [2 sc in next st, sc in next st] to last st, 2 sc in last st. Fasten off, leaving a long tail. (9 sts)

Sew ears to head.

Legs (make 2)

With A, make a magic ring.

Round 1: Ch 1 in ring, work 6 sc in ring, join with a sl st in top of first sc. (6 sts)

Round 2: Ch 1, 2 sc in each st around, join with a sl st in top of first sc. Fasten off A. (12 sts)

Round 3: Join B with a sl st, ch 1, sc in first st, [2 sc in next st, sc in next st] to last st, 2 sc in last st, join with a sl st in top of first sc. (18 sts)

Round 4: Ch 1, sc in each st around, join with a sl st in top of first sc. Fasten off B.

Round 5: Join C with a sl st, ch 1, sc in first 2 sts, [2 sc in next st, sc in next 2 sts] to last st, 2 sc in last st, join with a sl st in top of first sc. (24 sts)

Round 6: Ch 1, sc in each st around, join with a sl st in top of first sc. Fasten off C.

Rounds 7 and 8: Join D with a sl st, ch 1, sc in each st around, join with a sl st in top of first sc. Fasten off D at end of round 8.

Round 9: Join E with a sl st, ch 1, sc in first 6 sts, [sc2tog, sc in next 6 sts] to last 2 sts, sc2tog, join with a sl st in top of first sc. (21 sts remain)

Round 10: Ch 1, sc in first 5 sts, [sc2tog, sc in next 5 sts] to last 2 sts, sc2tog, join with a sl st in top of first sc. Fasten off E, leaving a long tail. (18 sts remain)

Lightly stuff legs. Sew legs to body.

Arms (make 2)

With A, make a magic ring.

Round 1: Ch 1 in ring, work 6 sc in ring, join with a sl st in top of first sc. (6 sts)

Round 2: Ch 1, 2 sc in each st around, join with a sl st in top of first sc. Fasten off A. (12 sts)

Rounds 3 and 4: Join B with a sl st, ch 1, sc in each st around, join with a sl st in top of first sc. Fasten off B at end of round 4.

Rounds 5 and 6: Join C with a sl st, ch 1, sc in each st around, join with a sl st in top of first sc. Fasten off C at end of round 6.

Rounds 7 and 8: Join D with a sl st, ch 1, sc in each st around, join with a sl st in top of first sc. Fasten off D at end of round 8, leaving a long tail.

Lightly stuff arms. Sew arms to body.

Tail

With A, make a magic ring.

Round 1: Ch 1 in round, work 8 sc in ring, join with a sl st in top of first sc. (8 sts)

Round 2: Ch 1, [sc2tog] 4 times, join with a sl st in top of first sc. Fasten off, leaving a tail.

Lightly stuff tail. Sew tail to body.

Right Strap

Foundation ch: With B, ch 5.

Row 1: Beg in second ch from hook, work hdc in each ch across. Fasten off, leaving a long tail. (4 sts)

Sew button on one end of strap, and sew other end of strap to right arm.

Left Strap

Foundation ch: With B, ch 25.

Row 1: Beg in eighth ch from hook (to create buttonhole), work sc in next 18 ch, ch 1 and turn. (18 sts)

Row 2: Sl st in next 18 sts, work 8 sc around buttonhole, continue along other edge, sl st in in each st to end. Fasten off, leaving a long tail. (44 sts)

TO FINISH

Sew end of strap without buttonhole to left arm. Weave in any remaining ends.

TECHNIQUES

Tools and Materials

YARN

Before you start a project, you will need to decide which type of yarn you would like to use: animal, plant, or synthetic. Each type of yarn fiber has its own unique characteristics. Wool, for instance (animal), is warm and absorbent but requires careful washing and drying. Cotton, bamboo, hemp, and linen (plant) are lightweight and breathe well. They are easier to wash and work well for warm-weather garments. Synthetic fibers, like acrylic and polyester, are the cheapest of the yarn options. They are machine-washable, making them the most popular choice for beginners.

Yarn also comes in various different weights (or "thicknesses") and the names for these weights differs from country to country. To make sure that you are using the correct yarn weight, check the ball band of your yarn for a recommended hook size and gauge, and compare that to the gauge specified in the pattern. Working up a gauge swatch is also a good idea.

YARN WEIGHTS

Yarn-weight symbol and category name	Super Fine	Fine	Light	Medium	Bulky	Super Bulky
Types of yarn in category	Sock, Fingering, Baby	Sport, Baby	DK, Light, Worsted	Worsted, Afghan, Aran	Chunky, Craft, Rug	Bulky, Roving
Crochet tension ranges* in Single Crochet to 10 cm	21 to 32 sts	16 to 20 sts	12 to 17 sts	11 to 14 sts	8 to 11 sts	5 to 9 sts
Recommended hook in metric size range	2.25 to 3.5 mm	3.5 to 4.5 mm	4.5 to 5.5 mm	5.5 to 6.5 mm	6.5 to 9 mm	9 mm and larger
Recommended hook in US size range	B-1 to E-4	E-4 to 7	7 to I-9	I-9 to K-10½	K-10½ to M-13	M-13 and larger

*These are guidelines only. They reflect the most commonly used tensions and needles or hook sizes for specific yarn categories.

CROCHET HOOKS

Crochet hooks are available in many different materials, shapes, and sizes. Depending on your grip (see Holding Your Hook, page 104), you might find one type of hook more comfortable than another. Ergonomic hooks, for example, are great for people who have wrist pain.

Keep in mind that some materials work better with specific yarns. Wooden hooks work well with slippery yarns, like Merino, but not so well with acrylics or synthetic yarns.

Some hooks also have blunter tips than others, making them better to use with yarn that splits, such as cotton.

SCISSORS, TAPESTRY NEEDLE, STITCH MARKERS, AND PINS

A small pair of scissors with sharp blades should be used to cut your yarn ends. Take care that you do not accidentally cut your work!

When sewing in yarn tails, use a blunt tapestry needle with a large eye. A blunt needle will help prevent working between the fibers of the yarn.

Stitch markers are useful for a number of reasons. They can be used to mark the start of a round or to mark the start of individual repeats within a round. Not only can they save you a lot of counting, but they can also save you ripping out a lot of stitches (known as frogging). If you do not have stitch markers, use a piece of scrap yarn to mark your stitches instead.

When sewing motifs together, you might find it useful to use pins to keep the motifs together while you work. Use rust-proof pins with large heads.

HOOK SIZES

All of the projects in this book use hooks smaller than US 15 N/P (10 mm). Hook sizes are specified at the start of each pattern.

GAUGE/TENSION

For many of the projects in this book, gauge is not important. Some projects will need to be made with a tight gauge, such as cushions to be stuffed, while other projects, like garments, will need to be made to an exact gauge. In these cases, it's important that you work up a gauge swatch first to check the appearance, density, and size of your work.

If you find that using the specified hook for any particular pattern makes your work too loose or lacy, try going down a hook size. If your work is too tight or dense, try going up a hook size.

ABBREVIATIONS

The patterns in this book feature a number of standard terms and abbreviations which are listed below.

beg	beginning
BLO	back loop only
BP	back post
CC	contrasting color
ch	chain
cl	cluster
dc	double crochet
dc2tog	double crochet next 2 sts together
FLO	front loop only
FP	front post
MC	main color
patt	pattern
pc	popcorn
rep	repeat
RS	right side
sc	single crochet
sc2tog	single crochet next 2 sts together
sl st	slip stitch
sp(s)	spaces
st(s)	stitches
tch	turning chain
tr2tog	treble next 2 sts together
WS	wrong side
yo	yarn over
yoke	the shaped area of the neckline and shoulders in a garment

Starting to Crochet

HOLDING YOUR HOOK

People generally hold their hook in one of two ways, the knife hold or the pencil hold. You can use whichever method you find most comfortable. You should hold your hook in your dominant hand while the non-dominant hand holds the yarn and controls the tension of your yarn.

Knife Hold

Hold your hook as you would hold your knife when you are eating. Most hooks have a flat surface called a thumb-rest; the tip of your thumb should be pressed flat against the thumb-rest.

Pencil Hold

Hold your hook as if you are holding a pencil. Your thumb sits on the thumb-rest, and the tip of your forefinger supports the back of the hook.

HOLDING YOUR YARN

There are lots of different ways to hold your yarn. Below are the two main options, woven and forefinger.

Woven

Weave the yarn through your fingers as shown: over your index finger, under your middle finger, and over your ring finger. If this feels too loose, wrap the yarn around your little finger once, like a ring.

Forefinger

Wrap the yarn around your forefinger twice.

SLIP KNOT

Place the end of the yarn in your left palm (right if you are left-handed) and hold it in place with your pinkie and ring finger. Wrap the yarn clockwise around your forefinger so that the working yarn crosses over the tail of yarn and forms a loop. Insert your hook into the loop, catch the working tail of yarn with your hook, and pull it through the loop. Hold both ends of yarn and pull them tight, but not too tight, until the slip knot rests against your hook.

CHAIN STITCH AND FOUNDATION CHAIN

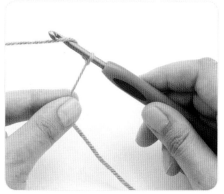

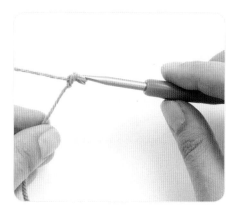

1. With a slip knot on your hook, hold the non-working end of the yarn between your thumb and middle finger. Swing your hook from front to back UNDER the working yarn so that the working yarn forms a "loop" over your hook. This is known as a yarn over. Still holding the non-working end, pull it slightly away from the hook.

2. Pull the loop created by the yarn over through the loop that is already on your hook. Make sure that the hook is pointing downward, otherwise it will catch on the loop that is already on your hook. You have now made your first chain stitch.

TURNING CHAINS

Turning chains are used to bring the start of a row/round up to the necessary height so that the top of the turning chain is in line with the tops of the rest of the stitches. The turning chain usually replaces the first stitch, but not always. Slip stitches do not require a turning chain. Single crochet stitches require one turning chain, but it is not counted as a stitch. Half-double crochet stitches require two turning chains; this ch-2 is counted as your first stitch. Double crochet stitches require three turning chains; this ch-3 is counted as as your first stitch. Treble crochet requires four turning chains; this ch-4 is counted as your first stitch. Please note that there are always exceptions to these general rules so read the individual pattern carefully.

Basic Stitches

SLIP STITCH (SL ST)

Slip stitches do not add any height to your work. They are usually used to join rounds. They can also be used to join separate pieces of fabric together or to reinforce an edge.

To make a slip stitch into the foundation chain, insert your hook into top loop only of the second chain from the hook. Wrap the yarn over the hook and pull through both loops on your hook.

To make a slip stitch in subsequent rows/rounds, insert your hook into both loops of the indicated stitch. Yarn over and pull through both loops on your hook.

SINGLE CROCHET (SC)

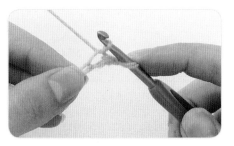

1. Insert your hook into the top loop only of the second chain from the hook.

2. Yarn over by swinging your hook from front to back UNDER the working yarn. Pull up a loop. You will now have 2 loops on your hook.

3. Pull through both loops on your hook to complete the first single crochet. Insert your hook into the next stitch and repeat Steps 2 and 3. Repeat until you have worked into every chain stitch in the foundation chain.

4. To make the next row, make one (turning) chain, then turn your work. Insert your hook under both loops of the first stitch and repeat Steps 2 and 3. Repeat for each stitch across. Your last single crochet should fall in the first single crochet of the previous round. Do not work into the turning chain.

HALF-DOUBLE CROCHET (HDC)

1. Yarn over and insert your hook into the top loop only of the third chain from the hook.

2. Yarn over again and pull up a loop. There should now be 3 loops on your hook.

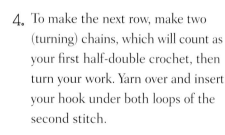

3. Yarn over again and pull through all 3 loops on your hook to complete your first half-double crochet. Yarn over, insert your hook into the next stitch, and repeat Steps 2 and 3. Repeat until you have worked into every chain stitch in the foundation chain.

4. To make the next row, make two (turning) chains, which will count as your first half-double crochet, then turn your work. Yarn over and insert your hook under both loops of the second stitch.

5. Complete Steps 2 and 3. Repeat for each stitch across the row. Your last half-double crochet should fall in the second chain of the turning ch-2 at the start of the previous row.

PLEASE NOTE

Occasionally a designer won't count this turning ch-2 as a stitch. In that case, you will make your first stitch in the top loop of the first stitch, and your last stitch will fall in the last half-double crochet, not in the top of the turning ch-2. To avoid confusion, follow the pattern instructions meticulously and count your stitches at the end of each row/round.

DOUBLE CROCHET (DC)

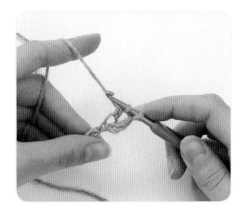

1. Yarn over and insert your hook into the top loop only of the fourth chain from the hook.

2. Yarn over again and pull up a loop. There should now be 3 loops on your hook.

3. Yarn over again and pull through 2 loops. There should now be 2 loops on your hook.

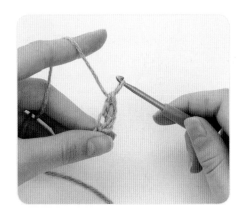

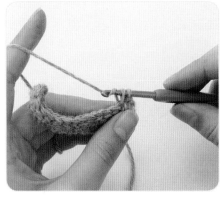

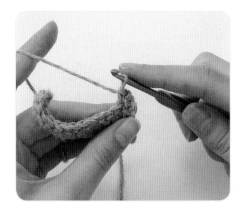

4. Yarn over and pull through both remaining loops on your hook to complete your first double crochet. Yarn over, insert your hook into the next stitch, and repeat Steps 2 to 4. Repeat into every chain stitch in the foundation chain.

5. To make the next row, make three (turning) chains, which will count as your first double crochet, then turn your work.

6. Yarn over and insert your hook under both loops of the second stitch. Complete steps 2 to 4.

TREBLE CROCHET (TR)

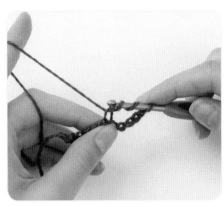

1. Yarn over twice and insert your hook into the top loop only of the fifth chain from the hook.

2. Yarn over again and pull up a loop. There should now be 4 loops on your hook.

3. (Yarn over and pull through 2 loops) three times to complete your first treble crochet.

4. To make the next treble crochet, yarn over twice, insert your hook into the next stitch, and repeat Steps 2 to 3. Repeat until you have worked into every chain stitch in the foundation chain.

5. To make the next row, make four (turning) chains, which will count as your first treble crochet, and turn your work. Yarn over twice and insert your hook under both loops of the second stitch. Complete steps 2 to 3. Repeat for each stitch across. Your last treble crochet should fall in the fourth chain of the turning ch-4 at the start of the previous row.

Increasing and Decreasing

INCREASING

Whether you are using single crochet, half-double crochet, double crochet, or treble crochet, the method remains the same.

To increase by one stitch at the beginning, middle, or end of a row/round, simply make 2 stitches in the same stitch.

DECREASING

Single Crochet Decrease (sc2tog)

1. Insert your hook through both loops of the indicated stitch and pull up a loop. Insert your hook into the next stitch and pull up a loop. There should now be 3 loops on your hook.

2. Yarn over and pull through all 3 loops.

Half-double Crochet Decrease (hdc2tog)

1. Yarn over and insert your hook through both loops of the indicated stitch. Yarn over and pull up a loop. Yarn over and insert your hook into the next stitch. Yarn over and pull up a loop. There should now be 5 loops on your hook.

2. Yarn over and pull through all 5 loops.

Double Crochet Decrease (dc2tog)

1. Yarn over and insert your hook through both loops of the indicated stitch. Yarn over and pull up a loop. Yarn over and pull through 2 loops. There should now be 2 loops on your hook. Yarn over and insert your hook into the next stitch. Yarn over and pull up a loop. Yarn over and pull through 2 loops on your hook. There should now be 3 loops on your hook.

2. Yarn over and pull through all 3 loops. Occasionally you will need to make a dc2tog at the very start of a row/round. In these instances you will ch 2 and dc in the next st. This will count as your Beginning Double Crochet Decrease (Beg Dc2tog).

Special Stitches

POST STITCHES

Front Post Stitches

Identify the post of the stitch you want to work around. Insert your hook from the front to the back and then from the back to the front around the post so that the post lies on top of your hook. Complete your stitch as normal.

Back Post Stitches

Back post stitches are a bit trickier than front post stitches, but once you get the hang of them you will love them!

1. Identify the post of the stitch you want to work around. Insert your hook from the back to the front and then from the front to the back around the post so that the post lies behind your hook.

2. Complete your stitch as normal. You might find it easier to twist your work forward to see what you are doing.

Loop Stitch

The loop stitch is a variation of single crochet that creates loops on the wrong side of your work.

1. Hold your work as you normally would, with your hook in the one hand and your other hand supporting both your work and yarn. Insert your hook into the next stitch.

2. Form a loop of yarn around the index finger of your non-hook hand.

3. Pass the hook behind both strands of this loop and catch the far side of the loop.

4. Pull this side through your stitch as you normally would when pulling up a loop, being careful to keep the loop around your index finger. You should have 2 loops on your hook.

5. Yarn over and pull through both loops to complete the stitch.

6. Repeat this for every loop stitch.

FRONT LOOP ONLY STITCHES (FLO)

Just like with chain stitches, the top of each single crochet, half-double crochet, double crochet, and treble crochet forms a "V."

Front loop only stitches are made by inserting your hook into the front loop only, not through both loops. The front loop will always be the one closest to you when you are holding your work.

BACK LOOP ONLY STITCHES (BLO)

Back loop only stitches are made by inserting your hook into the back loop only, not through both loops. The back loop will always be the one farthest away from you when you are holding your work.

STANDING SC

1. Start by making a slip knot on your hook with the new yarn.

4. Pull up a loop.

2. Insert your hook into the indicated stitch or space.

3. Yarn over the hook.

5. Yarn over the hook again.

6. Pull through both loops on the hook.

PLEASE NOTE

To make a standing hdc, wrap the yarn around the hook once and then simply follow the instructions for standing dc, but at step 4, pull through the first three loops on the hook. Once you are left with one loop on the hook, your standing hdc is complete and you can continue with the pattern.

STANDING DC

1. Wrap the yarn around the hook twice.

2. Insert your hook into the indicated stitch or space. Yarn over the hook.
3. Pull up a loop.
4. Yarn over and pull through the first two loops on the hook.

5. Yarn over and pull through the remaining two loops on the hook.

SPIKE STITCH

1. Insert the hook through the designated stitch two or more rows below. The number of rows down will determine how long the spike stitch is.

2. Draw the yarn through the stitch and back up to the working level.

3. Yarn over (yo) and draw the yarn through the 2 loops on your hook.

4. Continue to work until you are ready to add another spike stitch.

Working in the Round

When you work in the round, there are three methods with which to start. These are interchangeable, so use whichever method you prefer. When substituting methods, make sure that your stitch count is correct at the end of the first round.

MAKING YOUR FIRST ROUND INTO ONE CHAIN

This is the easiest of the 3 methods. You will need to start with a turning chain + 1. For example, if your first round is double crochet, you will need 4 chains (turning chain of 3 + 1 extra). The turning chain will count as your first stitch. The extra stitch will be your center and all the other stitches for the round will be made into it.

For example, ch 4. Make 11 double crochet stitches into the fourth chain from the hook. This will give you a stitch count of 12 for your first round.

"RING OF CHAINS"

This method works well if your first round has a lot of stitches because you can make a bigger "Ring of Chains" to accommodate them without bunching or overlapping. This method does leave a hole in the middle of your work, though, so if you want a tight center, use one of the other two methods.

You will need to start with a short chain. Join this chain into a ring by making a slip stitch into the chain farthest away from your hook. Make the required turning chain and then work the remainder of the round into this ring.

For example, ch 6. Join to the first chain with a sl st to form a ring. Ch 3 (this counts as your first double crochet). Make 11 double crochet stitches into the ring. This gives you a stitch count of 12 for your first round.

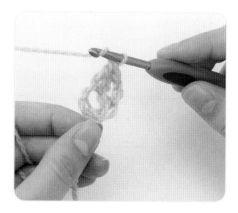

TIP

When using this method, work over your initial tail of yarn as you go. You can then pull on this tail of yarn once the round is complete to close the central hole. Make sure that you work this tail away securely to prevent the center from opening up again.

MAGIC RING

The magic ring is the trickiest of the three methods, but it is the most versatile. It can either yield a completely closed center, or accommodate as many stitches as you need.

For example, ch 3 (this counts as your first double crochet). Make 11 double crochet stitches into the magic ring. This will give you a stitch count of 12 for your first round.

When using this method, it is extremely important that you work your initial tail of yarn away very securely. If it comes undone, your whole project might unravel.

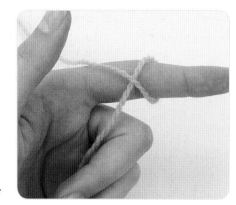

1. Place the end of the yarn in your left palm (right if you are left-handed) and hold it in place with your pinkie and ring finger. Wrap the yarn clockwise around your forefinger so that the working yarn crosses over the tail of yarn and forms a loop.

2. Remove the loop from your finger and hold it by pinching the point where the two strands of yarn overlap.

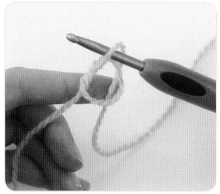

3. Insert your hook into the loop, catch the working tail of yarn with your hook, and pull it through the loop.

4. Yarn over and make a chain stitch to secure your working yarn. Make the required turning chain and work the remainder of the round into the magic ring. Remember to work over the initial tail of yarn as well. Close the hole by pulling on the initial tail of yarn.

INVISIBLE JOIN

1. Once you have made all the required stitches for the round, cut your yarn, leaving about a 4" tail, and pull this tail all the way through the top of the last stitch made. Now pick up your yarn needle and thread it with the tail of yarn. Insert your needle under both loops of the second stitch of the round. Pull the yarn tight, but not too tight.

2. Insert your needle into the top of the last stitch made. You want to insert it straight down into the eye formed by the loops. Make sure that you insert your needle through the third loop behind the stitch as well.

3. Pull your yarn through. This will form a "false" stitch. Make sure that you don't pull it too tight. You want this "false" stitch to be more or less the same size as your other stitches. To secure this stitch, insert your needle from top to bottom into the third loop behind the stitch and pull the yarn through again. Now work away your tails of yarn (see Weaving in Tails).

JOINING WITH A SLIP STITCH

1. Insert your hook into the first stitch of the round, remembering that the turning chain counts as a stitch.

2. Yarn over and pull through both the stitch and the loop on your hook to create a sl st. Work away your tails of yarn.

Changing Colors

You can use this method to join your new color (or a new ball of yarn) at the beginning or the middle of a row/round.

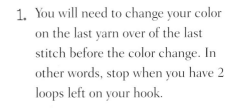

1. You will need to change your color on the last yarn over of the last stitch before the color change. In other words, stop when you have 2 loops left on your hook.

2. Let go of the old color and pick up the new color. Draw the new color through both loops to complete the stitch and continue as normal.

Finishing Your Work

FASTENING OFF

When you have made your last stitch, cut the yarn about 4" away from your work.

1. Pull on your hook to create a large loop and then remove your hook. Thread the tail of yarn through this loop.

2. Pull the yarn tight to fasten off. It will create a knot. Work away your tails of yarn (see Weaving in Tails).

WEAVING IN TAILS

A pattern will usually tell you to work away your "loose ends" or tails of yarn at the end. To do that, you need a blunt tapestry needle and a pair of scissors.

Thread the tapestry needle with the tail of yarn. Working on the wrong side of the fabric, thread your needle through at least 2" of stitches. Pull the yarn through all the way. Working in the opposite direction, and skipping the first stitch, insert your needle back into the same stitches again. Skipping the first stitch is essential, because it gives the yarn something to grip on to. Pull the yarn through again. Cut the yarn close to your work, being careful not to cut one of your stitches. If you have done this neatly, your tails won't be visible on the front of your work.

BLOCKING

Sometimes projects require blocking. This makes sewing individual pieces together easier, and creates a neat finish. You can either wet block or steam block.

Wet blocking

This method is suitable for all types of yarn. Pin the piece to the correct size (with the right side facing up), or pin it out so that it is tight but not too stretched. Using a spray bottle, mist the piece with cold water until it is damp but not wet. Allow the pieces to dry completely before removing the pins.

Steam blocking

Steam blocking is best suited to natural fibers like wool and cotton, as it is easy to accidentally melt your work if you are using synthetic fibers like acrylic. Pin the piece out on your ironing board, making sure that it is tight but not stretched out, and put your iron on the steam setting. Keep the iron about an inch above your work and blast it with steam, so that the steam penetrates the fibers without the iron touching the yarn. Leave to dry for at least 30 minutes and remove the pins.

SEAMS, JOINING, AND DETAIL

Whip Stitch

This stitch works really well on straight edges, such as when sewing the panels of a bag or cushion together.

With the right sides of the fabric pieces held together, insert the yarn needle from the front to the back of a stitch and through the corresponding stitch on the other piece. Bring the needle to the front again and repeat until the seam is finished.

Running Stitch

Running stitch is used to attach appliqué pieces to your work and has a decorative dotted-line appearance.

With the right side of your work facing you, insert your yarn needle from front to back into the indicated stitch and pull through. Insert your needle from back to front into the next stitch and pull through. Continue in this way until you have attached the required piece of appliqué.

AFTERCARE

Now that you have made your projects, it is important to care for them correctly.

If you have used acrylic yarn, caring for your pieces is fairly straightforward. You can wash them in the washing machine and dry them as you would any other easy-care garment. You might find that your pieces start pilling after a couple of uses/washes. This is easily remedied by running a dry shaving razor over the surface to get rid of any pilling. Please be gentle if you decide to do this, as you just want to remove pilling, not shave the actual yarn. Do not iron your pieces as this will "kill" (melt) the yarn.

If you have used plant fibers, such as cotton or linen, wash and dry as you would any garment. You can also iron your pieces if you wish, too.

If you have used animal fibers, such as wool, wash your items by hand and roll them in a towel to remove most of the moisture. Then lay them out flat to dry, shaping them as required. If you notice any pilling, gently scrape a dry razor over the surface to remove the pilling. Woolen items tend to pill less over time, unlike acrylic items which will keep on pilling.

Index

Yarns Used in the Projects

Rainbow Band Booties

Scheepjes Merino Soft; 50% Wool/ 25% Acrylic/25% Microfiber, 1.76 oz/50 g, 115 yds/105 m.

* 1 ball in C1 606 Da Vinci. Small amounts in each of the following colors: C2 615 Soutine, C3 646 Miro, C4 621 Picasso, C5 644 Duerer, C6 635 Matisse.

Gumdrops Pullover

Cascade Avalon; 50% Cotton/ 50% Acrylic, 3.5 oz /100 g, 175 yds/160 m.

* 2 [2, 2] balls in A 20 Heather. Small amounts in each of the following colors: B 14 Golf Green, C 09 Bird of Paradise, D 18 Turkish Sea, E 10 Artisan's Gold, F 27 Raspberry.

Ombré Socks

Debbie Bliss Baby Cashmerino; 55% Wool/33% Acrylic/12% Cashmere, 1.75 oz/50 g, 137 yds/125 m.

* 1 ball in each of the following colors:

Blue socks

A 100 White, B 204 Baby blue, C 071 Pool, D 059 Mallard.

Yellow socks

A 100 White, B 001 Primrose, C 091 Acid Yellow, D 083 Butter.

Little Flowers Playsuit

Drops Alpaca Silk Bushed; 100% Alpaca, 1.8 oz/50 g, 183 yds/167 m.

* 1 [2] balls in 100 Off White. Small amounts in each of the following colors:

Colorful Cardigan

Scheepjes Softfun; 60% Cotton/ 40% Acrylic, 1.76 oz/50 g, 153 yds/140 m.

* 3 balls in MC 2412. 1 ball in each of the following colors: CC1 2410, CC2 2518, CC3 2517, CC4 2452, CC5 2463.

Bright Striped Sun Hat

Scheepjes Softfun; 60% Cotton/ 40% Acrylic, 1.76 oz/50 g, 153 yds/140 m.

* 2 balls in MC 2412. Small amounts in each of the following colors: CC1 2410, CC2 2518, CC3 2517, CC4 2452, CC5 2463.

Citrus Diaper Cover

Scheepjes Softfun; 60% Cotton/ 40% Acrylic, 1.76 oz/50 g, 153 yds/140 m.

* 1 ball in each of the following colors: A 2518, B 2412, C 2410, D 2427, E 2517.

Snuggly Monster Mitts

Scheepjes Softfun; 60% Cotton/ 40% Acrylic, 1.76 oz/50 g, 153 yds/140 m.

* 1 ball in MC 2412. Small amounts in each of the following colors: CC1 2410, CC2 2518, CC3 2517, CC4 2452, CC5 2463.

Spring Stripes Dress

Scheepjes Catona; 100% Cotton, 69 yds/63 m, 0.88oz/25 g.

* 3 [4] balls in A 100 Lemon Chiffon. B 256 Cornelia Rose, C 222 Tulip, D 385 Crystalline.

Spring Stripes Leggings

Scheepjes Catona; 100% Cotton, 69 yds/63 m, 0.88 oz/25 g.

* 2 balls in A 100 Lemon Chiffon. B 256 Cornelia Rose, C 222 Tulip, D 385 Crystalline.

Walk in the Park Hoodie

Lion Brand Vanna's Choice Baby; 100% acrylic, 170 yds/155 m, 3.5 oz/100 g.

* 2 balls in A 108 Bluebell. 1 ball in B 139 Berrylicious. Small amount in C 157 Duckie.

Hot Air Balloon Bunting

Scheepjes Catona; 100% Cotton, 69 yds/63 m, 0.88 oz/25 g.

* 1 ball in each of the following colors: A 258 Rosewood, B 208 Yellow Gold,
* C 391 Deep Ocean Great, D 282 Ultra Violet, E 173 Bluebell, F 205 Kiwi.

Little Bear Rattle

Scheepjes Catona; 100% Cotton, 69 yds/63 m, 0.88 oz/25 g.

* 1 ball in each of the following colors: A 179 Topaz, B 146 Vivid Blue, C 397 Cyan, D 280 Lemon, E 281 Tangerine, F 256 Cornelia Rose.

Friendly Soft Toys

Scheepjes Stone Washed; 78% cotton/ 22% acrylic, 142 yds/130 m, 1.75 oz/50 g.

Bunny

* 2 balls in A 818 Lilac Quartz. 1 ball in each of the following colors: B 821 Pink Quartzite, F 811 Deep Amethyst. Small amount in C 813 Amazonite, D 820 Rose Quartz, E 819 New Jade.

Dog

* 2 balls in E 819 New Jade. 1 ball in D 820 Rose Quartz. Small amounts in each of the following colors: A 818 Lilac Quartz, C 813 Amazonite, D 820 Rose Quartz, F 811 Deep Amethyst.

Textured Stacking Blocks

Sheepjes Softfun; 60% Cotton/ 40% Acrylic, 153 yds/140 m, 1.75 oz/50 g.

* 1 ball in each of the following colors: A 2410, B 2511, C 2427, D 2516, E 2495, F 2518, G 2532.

Sunny Day Headband

Scheepjes Catona; 100% Cotton, 69 yds/63 m, 0.88 oz/25 g.

* 1 ball in A 130. Small amounts in each of following colors: B 115, C 280, D 205, E 400. Cloud Small amount of F 173.
* Sun Small amount of G 208.

Pastel Chevron Hat

Scheepjes Softfun Denim; 60% cotton/40% acrylic, 153 yds/140 m, 1.75 oz/50 g.
* 1 ball in A 2412. Small amounts of each of the following colors: B 504, C 512, D 509, E 516, F 518.

Pastel Chevron Mittens

Scheepjes Softfun Denim; 60% cotton/40% acrylic, 153 yds/140 m, 1.75 oz/50 g.
* 1 ball in A 2412. Small amounts in each of the following colors: B 504, C 512, D 509, E 516, F 518.

Gradient Floor Blanket

Cascade 220 Superwash; 100% Wool, 220 yds/200 m, 3.5 oz/100 g.
* 4 balls in A 871 White. 1 ball in each of the following colors : B 809 Really Red, C 825 Orange, D 821 Daffodil, E 820 Lemon, F 851 Lime, G 850 Lime Sherbert, H 848 Blueberry, I 844 Periwinkle, J 837 Berry Pink, K 835 Pink Rose, L 837 Very Berry, M 1973 Seafoam Heather, N 1969 Heather.

Pretty Mary Janes

Drops Paris; 100% cotton, 82 yds/75 m, 1.75 oz/50 g.
* 1 ball in each of the following colors: A 17 Off White, B 31 Medium Purple.
* Small amounts in each of the following colors: E 19 Light Yellow, F 01 Apricot.
Drops Cotton Light; 50% Cotton/50% Polyester, 115 yds/105 m, 1.8 oz/50 g.
* Small amounts in each of the following colors: C 08 Ice Blue, D 11 Green.

Bobble Pacifier Cords

Cascade 220 Superwash; 100% Wool, 220 yds/200 m, 3.5 oz/100 g.
* 1 ball in MC 871 White.
* Small amount in one of the following colors : 825 Orange, 820 Lemon, 851 Lime, 837 Berry Pink, 1973 Seafoam Heather, 1969 Heather.

Whatever the Weather Wall Hanging

Bernat Super Value; 100% Acrylic, 425 yds/389 m, 7 oz/197 g.
* Small amounts in each of the following colors: A 445 White, B 615 Yellow, C 615 Carrot, D 610 Royal Blue, E 246 Lush, F 517 True Red, G 520 Cool Blue.
Cascade 220 Solid; 100% Wool, 220 yds/200 m, 3.5 oz/100 g.
* Small amount in H 7827 Goldenrod.

Climbing Colors Blanket

Red Heart Baby Hugs Medium; 100% Acrylic, 247 yds/225 m, 4.5 oz/127 g.
* 4 balls in 4001 A Frosting. 1 ball in each of the following colors: B 4909 Ladybug, C 4255 Orangie, D 4201 Sunny, E 4562 Aloe, F 4825 Bluie, G 4538 Lilac.

Mini Nesting Baskets

Scheepjes Stone Washed XL; 70% Cotton/30% Acrylic, 82 yds/75 m, 1.76 oz/50 g.
* 1 ball in each of the following colors: 847 Red Jasper, 856 Coral, 852 Lemon Quartz, 853 Amazonite.

Freddie Frog Bottle Cozy

Scheepjes Softfun; 60% Cotton/40% Acrylic, 153 yds/140 m, 1.76 oz/50 g.
* 1 ball in each of the following colors: A 2432, B 2519. Small amounts in each of the following colors: C 2516, D 2517, E 2518, F 2480, G 2412, H 2532.

Monster Pillow Cover

Scheepjes Stone Washed XL; 70% Cotton/30% Acrylic, 82 yds/75 m, 1.76 oz/50 g.
* 2 balls in A 853 Amazonite. 1 ball in each of the following colors: B 846 Canada Jade, C 856 Coral, D 857 Citrine, E 841 Moon Stone.

Fun-Shapes Organizer

Scheepjes Bloom; 100 Cotton, 87 yds/80 m, 1.76 oz/50 g.
* 4 balls in A 419 Forget-me-not. 1 ball in each of the following colors: B 413 Gerbera, C 408 Tiger Lily, D 406 Tulip, E 422 Old Lily, F 414 Sun Flower.

Drops Storage Basket

Scheepjes Roma Big; 144 yds/132 m, 7.76 oz/220 g.
* 3 balls in A 25. 1 ball in B 3.
Scheepjes Catona; 100% Cotton, 69 yds/63 m, 0.88 oz/25 g.
* Small amounts in each of the following colors: C 258 Rosewood, D 208 Yellow Gold, E 205 Kiwi, F 391 Deep Ocean Great, G 282 Ultra Violet.

Rainbow Waves Stroller Blanket

Scheepjes Merino Soft; 50% Wool/25% Acrylic/25% Microfiber, 1.76 oz/50 g, 115 yds/105 m.
* 2 balls in G 640 Warhol, H 645 van Eyck. 1 ball in each of the following colors: A 638 Hockney, B 602 Raphael, C 621 Picasso, D 614 Magritte, E 646 Miro, F 615 Soutine.

Buddy Bear Curtain Tie

Drops Cotton Light; 50% Cotton/50% Polyester, 115 yds/105 m, 1.75 oz/50 g.
* 1 ball in each of the following colors: A 25 Light Lilac, B 23 Light Purple, C 18 Pink, D 05 Light Pink, E 01 Off White.
Drops Love You 5; 100% Cotton, 115 yds/75 m, 1.75 oz/50 g. F 117 Purple.

Meet the Designers

KIRSTEN BALLERING

Ombré Socks 15 ∘ Gradient Floor Blanket 62 ∘ Bobble Pacifier Cords 69
Kirsten discovered crochet while living in Sweden and hasn't stopped creating since! She's passionate about designing colorful and functional projects and works from her studio in the Netherlands, where she lives together with her fiancé and cats. You'll never find her hands idle! Follow her blog on haakmaarraak.nl.

CAROLYN CHRISTMAS

Textured Stacking Blocks 50 ∘ Freddie Frog Bottle Cozy 78 ∘ Fun-Shapes Organizer 87
Carolyn started designing years ago after giving birth to twins. In the ensuing years, she has been a crochet designer, magazine and book editor, teacher, author, and publisher. Nowadays, she and her husband, David, live and work in their 100-year-old home in the Texas Hill Country. You can find Carolyn's designs at pinkmambo.com.

SOPHIE CORMIER

Little Flowers Playsuit 19 ∘ Whatever the Weather Wall Hanging 72
Sophie has been crocheting and designing for four years and knitting for seven. She lives on the beautiful east coast of Canada with her two children. Owner of *Illumikniti Designs* and a self-proclaimed yarn hoarder, she knits beautiful props for photographers. You can find her work and patterns at newbornprops.ca.

SHELLEY HUSBAND

Sunny Day Headband 55
Shelley is a long-time crafter whose current passion is designing crochet patterns. Her patterns gently encourage crocheters to extend their skills to create items they didn't think themselves able to do. She lives with her husband and teenage daughters in a tiny town on the coast of Victoria, Australia. Find all her patterns and tutorials on spincushions.com.

CARMEN JORISSEN

Little Bear Rattle 44 ∘ Friendly Soft Toys 47
Carmen is a designer specializing in cute amigurumi toys and quirky home decor items. She started her creative blog back in 2012 and in 2014 she was awarded the *Mollie Makes Youth Award*. Browse through her colorful Instagram feed at @crafty_queens and find free patterns on craftyqueens.nl.

DOROTEJA KARDUM

Rainbow Band Booties 8 ∘ Pretty Mary Janes 66 ∘ Buddy Bear Curtain Tie 96
Doroteja Kardum is the blogger and crochet designer behind *Croby Pattern Designs*. After learning to crochet a few years ago, it has since become the source of a lifestyle full of creativity and happiness. Doroteja's favorite things to crochet are baby clothes, shoes, and toys. You can find her creations on crobypatterns.com.

TATSIANA KUPRYIANCHYK

Rainbow Waves Stroller Blanket 93 ∘ Monster Pillow Cover 84
Tatsiana Kupryianchyk is a designer and the creative mind behind *Lilla Björn Crochet*. As well as focusing on home accessories and soft toys, Tatsiana is obsessed with mandala art, which allows her to spend long hours playing with yarns and learning new techniques. Find Tatsiana's designs at http://www.lillabjorncrochet.com and on Instagram at @lillabjorncrochet.

RHONDDA MOL

Colorful Cardigan 21 ∘ Bright
Striped Sun Hat 25 ∘ Snuggly
Monster Mitts 30 ∘ Pastel Chevron
Hat 57 ∘ Pastel Chevron Mittens 60
Rhondda is a freelance Crochet
Designer and a full-time Blogger at
Oombawka Design Crochet. Here she
shares her love of crochet with the
online crochet community through
her beginner-friendly free patterns
and tutorials. She currently resides in
Ontario, Canada with her husband
and two young children. Find her
patterns on Ravelry as RhonddaM
and follow her daily crochet blog at
oombawkadesigncrochet.com.

AMY RAMNARINE

Citrus Diaper Cover 27 ∘ Spring
Stripes Dress 32 ∘ Spring Stripes
Leggings 34 ∘ Whatever the Weather
Wall Hanging 72
Amy has been designing her own
crochet patterns professionally since
2012. Her creations are all made at
her home in New York, where she lives
with her husband, son, and daughter.
Amy loves to crochet, craft, and
create recipes. She shares her crochet
creations and crafting adventures on
her blog: thestitchinmommy.com.

PIA THADANI

Gumdrops Pullover 10 ∘
Walk in the Park Hoodie 36 ∘
Climbing Colors Blanket 76
Pia is the designer and blogger behind
StitchesNScraps.com. She is also
a member of the Crochet Guild of
America and has earned the Master
of Advanced Crochet Stitches &
Techniques designation. She loves
variety, so she enjoys creating different
kinds of designs and exploring new
techniques and stitch combinations.

DEDRI UYS

Hot Air Balloon Bunting 42 ∘
Mini Nesting Baskets 78 ∘
Drops Storage Basket 90
Dedri Uys is the author of *Big Hook
Rag Crochet* and *Amamani Puzzle
Balls*. Dedri is passionate about
crochet and shares her love of the
craft through online patterns and
tutorials. She lives in London with
her husband, three sons, and the
family cat. Find her patterns on
Ravelry at dedri-uys or follow her
blog at lookatwhatimade.net.

Acknowledgments

The publisher would like to thank the following for their help in making this book:

Dedri Uys, for her fantastic eye for design, crocheting expertise, and curatorial skills, which brought the designers together.

Thank you to the wonderful crocheters for designing and making the projects: Kirsten Ballering, Carolyn Christmas, Sophie Cormier, Shelley Husband, Carmen Jorissen, Doroteja Kardum, Tatsiana Kupryianchyk, Rhondda Mol, Amy Ramnarine, and Pia Thadani.

Many thanks to Scheepjeswol (www.scheepjes.com) for supplying the beautiful yarn for many of the projects.

Thank you to photographer Simon Pask, and our models Beau Raviraj, Sigraveana Connell, Gemma Hickingbotham, Maisen Hall, Martha Minter, and Kayden Rajoo for bringing the projects to life.

Thanks also to Therese Chynoweth, Lindsay Kaubi, Jen Riley, and Ann Barrett for their editorial work and index.

Rainbow Illustrations © NadineVeresk/Shutterstock.